BECOMING JEWISH

A Handbook for Conversion

Rabbi Ronald H. Isaacs

The Rabbinical Assembly
New York, New York

To all who are Jews by choice

For Ruthie, Doreen, Ron, Richard, Dorothy, Loren, Arnis
and Caryn

Contents

Preface

The telephone rings. An apprehensive voice asks for an appointment to discuss conversion to Judaism. The frequency of such calls has increased. I am always excited to meet with a prospective convert and hear his or her story.

Usually the first questions concern the length of time that conversion takes and details of the conversion process. It is no surprise that someone considering conversion would be interested in these things. Yet finding the answers, and simply getting started, can often be frustrating for the prospective convert.

This handbook outlines and answers some of the questions that converts frequently ask: What are the stages of conversion? Where do I begin? What do I have to learn? How will conversion affect my relationship with my family? How do I make a Jewish home?

This book is intended to answer your questions and to give you a better understanding of the feelings and inner conflicts that often emerge once the door to Judaism is opened. The appendix at the back of the book will be a useful guide both during and after your course of study. It contains information on the Jewish calendar, Jewish holidays, prayers, and Jewish history, a glossary of useful terms, and suggested readings for further study.

I am grateful to those who have shared in the labors of this book. My colleagues Rabbis Henry Glazer, Neil Kurshan, and Elie Spitz reviewed the manuscript and offered many useful suggestions. My friend Rabbi Jules Harlow, who is responsible for all Rabbinical Assembly publications, deserves thanks for his most appreciated comments and editorial skills. I also wish to thank Rabbi Simon Glustrom, chairman of the Rabbinical Assembly Publications Committee, for his interest in the project and his assistance in helping to make it a reality. Finally, this book has been enhanced by the guidance offered by several of my conversion students. Like so many other Jews by choice, they have enriched Jewish life with their enthusiasm for God and the Jewish way of holiness. They have become active members of their synagogues and local Jewish communal institutions, and have created authentically Jewish homes. Their assistance in preparing this handbook and their encouragement and dedication have been an inspiration to me and to many others who were born Jewish, and will prove equally inspiring to all who choose to open the door to our magnificent tradition. I shall always be grateful to them.

Ronald H. Isaacs
Erev Rosh HaShanah, 5753

1

Considering a New Identity

Entreat me not to leave you. For wherever you go, I will go; and where you lodge, I will lodge; your people shall be my people and your God my God.

—Ruth 1:16

Who converts and how many people have converted?

It is estimated that over ten thousand people convert to Judaism in the
United States every year. This number is unprecedented in modern
history. Many of these conversions occur prior to a marriage, some
after a marriage but prior to the birth of a child. Others are precipitated
by a desire for family togetherness and the need of people in love to
share every aspect of their lives with each other. Still others choose
Judaism out of a personal conviction that it provides the most
meaningful way of life for them, and that being a Jew is right for their
own sense of identity and the definition of their personality.

What does the Bible say about converts?

During the biblical period, before the destruction of the Temple in
Jerusalem (586 B.C.E.), the concept of conversion did not exist. When
Israelite men married non-Israelite women, their wives were expected
to worship the God of Israel. The wives became full members of the
Israelite nation. When Israelite women married non-Israelite men,
they joined their husbands' nation.

The Bible records many mixed marriages (i.e., marriages between
Israelites and non-Israelites). Moses, David, and Solomon married
non-Israelite women.

The most famous biblical mixed-marriage story concerns Ruth, a
Moabite woman who became an "Israelite by choice." Ruth was
married to an Israelite man who had settled in Moab. When he died,
she did not resume life as a Moabite, as would have been customary
in those days, but decided to accompany her mother-in-law, Naomi,
back to Israel. Naomi advised Ruth to stay in Moab, but Ruth
responded, "Entreat me not to leave you. For wherever you go, I will
go; and where you lodge, I will lodge; your people shall be my people
and your God my God" (Ruth 1:16). With these simple and beautiful
words, Ruth chose to become an Israelite. This was the first instance
in history of a "conversion" to Judaism not directly related to a
marriage. Since Ruth was an ancestor of King David, Israel's greatest
monarch and poet, and progenitor of the Messiah, we can see that the
Bible's view of conversion is quite positive.

When did the first conversions take place?

In the sixth century B.C.E. Jerusalem was conquered by the Babylonian king Nebuchadnezzar. During the period that followed, known as the Babylonian Exile, large numbers of Jews were forced to leave their homeland and live in Mesopotamia. Many people there were attracted to the Jewish religion and attached themselves to the Jewish people. The prophet Isaiah referred to them as "those who joined themselves to the Lord" (Isaiah 56:3-7), promising that they would be among the returnees to Zion. In 538 B.C.E. the Persian king Cyrus overran the Babylonian Empire and allowed the exiled Jews to return home. In the centuries that followed, during the period known as the Second Commonwealth, the Jewish people began to engage in extensive conversionary activities. Among the many Jews by choice in this era were members of the Roman aristocracy and the rulers of several Near Eastern principalities.

What did the ancient rabbis say about converts?

A convert, or proselyte, is someone who converts from one religion to another. Rabbinic opinions about proselytes are mixed and varied. One source declares: "Proselytes are as hard for Israel as a sore" (Talmud, *Yevamot* 47b). But we also find statements such as: "Beloved are proselytes by God, for the Bible everywhere uses the same epithet of them as of Israel" (Talmud, *Gerim* 4:3).

Today, authorities agree that anyone who chooses Judaism and fulfills the requirements for conversion shall be accepted as a full-fledged Jew and held in high regard. The following midrash says it best:

> Dearer to God than all of the Israelites who stood at Mount Sinai is the convert. Had the Israelites not witnessed the lightning, thunder, and quaking mountain, and had they not heard the sounds of the shofar, they would not have accepted the Torah. But the convert, who did not see or hear any of these things, surrendered to God and accepted the yoke of Heaven. Can anyone be dearer to God than such a person?
> —*Tanḥuma* (ed. Buber), *Lekh Lekha* 6.32

Why is marriage within the faith so important for Judaism?

Judaism stresses the importance of marrying within the faith and preserving its heritage of culture and traditions. Differences of religion often constitute a serious obstacle to harmonious husband-wife relationships. Even when mixed marriages endure, they often impose a strain on the religious loyalties of one or both partners, and cause difficult personal and family problems.

The earliest biblical story about the importance of marrying within the faith is related to Judaism's first patriarch, Abraham (Genesis 24). Abraham sends his servant Eliezer to find a suitable wife for his son Isaac, admonishing him with these words: "I will make you swear that you will not take a wife for my son from the daughters of the Canaanites among whom I dwell, but you will go to the land of my birth and get a wife for my son" (Genesis 24:3).

This is the first biblical reference on the subject of opposition to mixed marriage. Religion and family tradition are at stake, not ethnic or racial "purity."

In another biblical story, Isaac charges his son Jacob not to take a wife from among the Canaanites, a non-Israelite people inhabiting ancient Palestine (Genesis 28:1). And who can forget the extreme bitterness of Isaac and Rebekah when they learn that their son Esau has taken Hittite wives (Genesis 26:34-35)?

If Abraham, Isaac, and Rebekah did not clearly explain why they were opposed to mixed marriages, no room is left for guesswork when the Book of Deuteronomy (7:3) restates the matter in legal terms. It warns the Israelites that when they come to the Promised Land and become acquainted with its inhabitants, they are not to intermarry with them, for that will turn their children away from God. The Bible is warning here that mixed marriages pose a threat to Jewish survival.

The strongest biblical denunciation of mixed marriages is found in the Book of Ezra, written soon after the return from the Babylonian Exile. The practice of mixed marriage had become quite common then. Ezra did not simply denounce it; he ordered all intermarried Jews to divorce their gentile wives (Ezra 9:12 ff.).

In summation, aside from the important consideration of marital harmony, Judaism opposes mixed marriage because it poses a threat to the future of the Jewish people, and to their faith, customs, and traditions. The Jewish people are and always have been a minority. Seeking to preserve their group identity, they find it crucial to resist the inroads of mixed marriage.

What are the advantages of a Jewish marriage?

There are many advantages to a Jewish marriage over a mixed marriage. You and your partner will be able to share the warmth and strength of Jewish customs and observances, song and prayer, food, literature, and the like, without the need for constant explanation and interpretation. When you become parents your children will not be torn between two religious traditions, nor will they be denied religious training because of conflicting beliefs which can sometimes lead to total avoidance. Growing up in a household with two faiths, and having to choose one over the other, is very difficult. When young people raised in mixed-marriage households set out to establish their own religious identities, they often feel as if they are being forced to choose one parent over the other.

In a Jewish marriage, the aspirations of the Jewish people as a whole become part of the shared goals of the two partners. Together they are able to fashion a moral life, participate in the religious and cultural life of our people, and help to rebuild the State of Israel, in the process building a richer and more secure basis for their own relationship.

Finally, by establishing a Jewish marriage you will be helping to assure the continuity of Judaism and the Jewish people.

What are the steps leading to conversion?

According to the Talmud, conversion entails:

1. Knowledge and acceptance of the Torah's commandments.

2. Circumcision (*brit milah*) for men, which is the physical sign of the covenant of Israel. (If a man has already been circumcised, *hatafat dam brit* is required to complete the ritual requirement. In this brief and simple rite, one drop of blood is drawn from the tip of the penis.)

3. Immersion in a pool of water known as a ritual bath (*mikvah*).

These three elements have been the basis of the traditional conversion ceremony for centuries, but they come as the culmination of a process that begins when the prospective proselyte first decides to set out on the road of conversion to Judaism.

Most converts go through a more or less similar sequence of emotional feelings. One of my students described it as follows:

1. *An "interest."* Brought about by my relationship with my partner.

2. *Casual learning.* I read six or seven basic books recommended by a family rabbi.

3. *Commitment to serious study.* This was when I went to see a sponsoring rabbi. We were talking about marriage and family, and we both felt strongly that a home should have one religion; and I knew I didn't want it to be the one in which I was raised.

4. *Decision.* I made the definite decision that I would convert several months after starting to study; it was during Passover.

5. *"Limbo."* This was the hardest part. Continuing to study and gaining confidence in my "Jewishness," but not really Jewish and not Christian. Holidays were very difficult. Christmas was miserable. I didn't celebrate in my home but I spent the day with my parents. And Simhat Torah was very hard because I couldn't have an *aliyah* with the rest of the congregation.

6. *"I'm ready."* When I finally came to my sponsoring rabbi to set the date. A great sense of anticipation.

7. *"The Big Day."* The actual day of my conversion—one of high emotions and anticipation.

2

Beginning a Program of Study

Rabbi Eleazar said: The Holy One only dispersed the Jews among the nations so that converts would join them.
—Talmud, *Pesaḥim* 87b

What are the initial steps in the conversion process?

There is no standardized conversion process in Conservative Judaism. Some common practices, however, are generally followed.

You should begin by seeking out a competent rabbi with whom to discuss your special situation, family background, and individual needs. If you or your partner's family are involved in a synagogue, the rabbi would be a good person with whom to initiate contact. If not, you may wish to call the local Conservative synagogue. If there are no synagogues nearby, call the Jewish Federation in your area or the Jewish studies department at a local college or university. Without doubt, one or another of these resources will be able to assist you in finding a suitable rabbi.

Many converts have emphasized the importance of this first step, especially reiterating their need to find a rabbi with whom they could talk openly. One convert stated it this way: "I felt that it was not only important to find a competent rabbi, but to find one with whom you are comfortable and to whom you can speak freely."

Be prepared at your first meeting to be asked many questions that will better acquaint the rabbi with your reasons for seeking conversion to Judaism. Do not expect to be accepted immediately as a candidate for conversion. (It is quite customary for a rabbi to inform you of the difficulties you are likely to face as a Jew and the challenging new responsibilities that you will need to assume. You may even feel discouraged.)

Be candid, sincere, and persistent. You may be asked to meet with the rabbi more than once. If the rabbi is convinced of your sincerity and honesty, and feels that you are a viable candidate, he or she will probably offer to be your sponsor. This means that you will have a personal teacher and facilitator who will take you through the process of conversion from beginning to end.

How long will my conversion take? What is the course of study?

How long it takes to convert is often determined by the conversion candidate's cognitive and emotional readiness. A year or more of study is common. It is likely that you will be asked to attend formal classes as well as private sessions with your sponsoring rabbi.

Whereas the formal classes will allow you an opportunity to engage in a group experience with other persons, your private sessions with your sponsoring rabbi will enable you to share your feelings and reactions to your learning experiences. In addition you will be able to ask your sponsoring rabbi to help clarify matters and answer questions which have arisen during your course of formal study.

The areas of study covered will include Hebrew language, Jewish history, holidays and prayers, and life-cycle events. In many larger cities throughout the United States and Canada, Conservative congregations have their own conversion classes. In some communities a conversion school is sponsored by a group of local rabbis or congregations. These schools generally have several faculty members and require you and your partner (should you have one) to attend. Your sponsoring rabbi will be able to provide you with information about schools and classes. Some sponsoring rabbis and conversion schools ask their candidates to keep a personal diary, noting what they have heard, tasted, smelled or experienced of Judaism that week. The contents of the diaries are often shared by the candidates during class discussion.

It is most advantageous to be a part of a group class experience. Having a peer group will allow you to share experiences throughout the conversion process.

How should I study?

Several rules of thumb will help to ensure a successful program. Regular attendance at all required classes, whether with your sponsoring rabbi or at the conversion school, and careful reading and preparation of your assignments are very important. Do not be afraid to ask questions when you have difficulty understanding something. This is all a part of the learning process. Really work at the Hebrew language—it is central to feeling comfortable and confident, especially when attending synagogue services.

It is likely that your sponsoring rabbi will ask you to attend services regularly. This provides a wonderful opportunity for you to familiarize yourself with prayers and customs, and to become acquainted with the local Jewish community.

Since Judaism is a family-centered, "hands-on" religion, it is never too late to begin to experience and participate in Jewish holiday celebrations or even to initiate your own special Jewish traditions for the celebration of holidays. Here again your sponsoring rabbi can assist you in networking with knowledgeable observant families who can share Jewish experiences of celebration with you. Make sure to attend a meaningful Passover Seder, listen to the reading of the Megillah (Scroll of Esther) on Purim, and hear the sounds of the shofar (ram's horn) on Rosh HaShanah. You may even want to try fasting on the Day of Atonement (Yom Kippur) to see what it feels like. Certainly you will want to experience the dancing and singing with the Torah scrolls on the joyous festival of Simhat Torah, and to light candles on Hanukkah. Remember that Shabbat, the holiest day of each week, is the perfect time for you to study, relax, pray, and familiarize yourself with some of the rituals of Judaism.

Begin to learn about and keep the Jewish dietary laws (*kashrut*). Judaism teaches the idea of reverence for all life in many different ways. One of these is by hallowing the act of eating and the special preparations which it entails. As you begin to observe the dietary laws, your Jewish identity will be further reinforced.

Finally, you will want to study and eventually experience through action the other *mitzvot* (commandments) that are required of the Jewish people. Judaism has always been, and continues to be, a vital religious way of life. As a people, Jews enjoy a sustaining relationship with God because we have chosen to accept God's laws. As one who is choosing Judaism, you have the responsibility to study God's laws, experience them, and then follow them.

As is clear from what we are told by people who have gone through the conversion process, students are more comfortable and less anxious about their conversions when they invest serious effort in experiencing various facets of Jewish life as early as possible.

What resources are available to me?

Your sponsoring rabbi and formal classes are among your best resources. Integration into the synagogue of your sponsoring rabbi is also an important step toward building a positive Jewish identity. Speaking to others in your conversion class or to people who have recently completed their courses of study, and sharing ideas and thoughts with them, can provide you with additional support. If there is a Jewish community center in your area you may also want to investigate its educational and cultural programs. Many college campuses have Jewish programming and Judaic studies programs. Jewish books, role models, friends, and surrogate Jewish families will also help you in your exploration of Judaism.

In addition to these resources, there is an abundance of other possible resources for your consideration. Here is a partial listing. You may wish to visit some of them or even to volunteer your time if you are so inclined.

1. Jewish book stores.
2. Jewish day schools.
3. Jewish homes for the aged.
4. Jewish bakeries.
5. Jewish meat markets.
6. Jewish museums.
7. Local bureaus of Jewish education.
8. Local branches of Jewish organizations like Hadassah, National Council of Jewish Women, B'nai B'rith, Temple Brotherhoods, Temple Sisterhoods, American Jewish Committee, and American Jewish Congress, among others.
9. Individuals who have converted to Judaism and are willing to discuss their experiences with you.

Involving yourself with some of these persons and organizations will undoubtedly open new doors of Jewish knowledge to you, and help you network with some very interesting Jewish people in the community.

3

Your Non-Jewish Family and Friends

If I am only for myself, what am I?
                    —*Ethics of the Fathers 1:14*

*H*ow will my conversion affect my relationship with my family?

Parents of converts often feel that they will be left out of their children's lives. They may fear rejection because of their lack of knowledge about Judaism. For this reason it is most important to explain to your family that you will still be the same person as before your conversion, except of course with a different religious orientation. You may also want to lovingly remind and assure them that you are and always will be their child—that they are not "losing" you, and you are not abandoning them. Be sure to tell them that they did nothing wrong in raising you, that you will always treasure your memories of childhood and family. By constantly communicating with your family and providing them with reassurances of your love, your relationship will likely remain a positive one.

How and when should I tell family and friends about my plans?

There is no single approach to when and how you should tell your parents about your conversion plans. You know your parents best, and ultimately you are the one who has to decide on the approach that will work best for you and them.

A few guidelines are in order when telling your parents of your plans. Remember, though, that these are only recommendations, based on what has worked well for some converts. Evaluate each one according to your own individual circumstances.

1. Tell your parents in person. Be honest and don't withhold information. Share your happiness and excitement—most parents can't argue with that.
2. Pick a time that will be free from distraction.
3. It is best not to tell your parents on special occasions like anniversaries, birthdays, or holidays. These days are high in emotional impact and therefore less suitable.
4. Be prepared to defend and explain your motivation for conversion. In most cases your parents will want to know your reasons.
5. Relax and remain calm. Reassure your family that your love for them is as strong as ever and that you are still their child and will always be a part of them.
6. Some converts continue the discussion with their parents in a

follow-up letter. If you decide to write such a letter, it may help you to clarify your position. It will also provide an opportunity for you to restate your devotion to your family.

7. Discuss your desire to convert more than once. Your family may not listen to your reasons for converting at first; they may be preoccupied by their own concerns or simply may need time to assimilate what you have told them. So tell them again. If they ignore your decision, wait patiently and continue to reassure them that you love them very much.

What reactions should I expect, and how should I deal with them?

Reactions to the news that a child intends to convert to Judaism will vary from family to family. Much depends on the general relationship between parents and child and the strength of the family's ties to its own religion.

In most cases, you should not expect your parents to react to the news with complete acceptance and total happiness. They will surely need time to get used to the idea. Sometimes parents are very unaccepting, possibly expressing total disapproval and even anger. A common reaction might be, "Why do you have to convert for him (her)? Why can't he (she) convert for you?" Some parents may feel guilt and a sense of personal rejection. Some may worry about how friends and other relatives (grandparents, aunts and uncles, cousins) will react to the news.

It is up to you to try to assuage your parents' fears, worries, and concerns. Constant communication and sharing of information are important ingredients in maintaining a healthy relationship between you and your family.

Time tends to heal. Try as best you can to be patient with yourself and your parents. Begin slowly to include them in some of your new celebrations. Do not expect them to immediately share in your enthusiasm, for it is you who are converting, and not they. Gradually educating them through family involvement may help enhance the similarities rather than emphasize the differences. Many converts report that with the passage of time, their parents have grown to accept and respect their religious differences.

4

Your Jewish Partner and Family

Set me as a seal upon your heart.

—*Song of Songs 8:6*

How will my future spouse feel about my conversion, and how will it affect our relationship?

A future spouse often is reserved about encouraging conversion out of fear of being blamed in the future if any harm to the relationship ensues. Once you have made it clear that you plan to convert to Judaism, your future partner will probably be pleased, knowing that you will now begin to build a Jewish life together, learning and sharing along the way. It is essential that the both of you engage in the learning process. Most if not all schools of conversion require that both partners be present in class. Often the born Jew will learn a great deal from the classes. In addition, attending together will enable you to be fully supportive of each other. It will also afford you increased opportunities to communicate with each other, clarifying issues and sharing feelings throughout the process.

As you become involved in the learning process and begin to develop a new identity as a Jew, you may feel that you want to do everything "right" and experience everything. You will feel anxious and eager to become observant. You may even want to initiate certain practices that your future spouse does not presently perform and may criticize him or her for not following a practice or custom that you think important. Your future spouse, on the other hand, may fear that you will become "too Jewish." Sometimes this will induce your future spouse to examine personal practices and attitudes, and to make decisions about what he or she is willing to do. Take time and learn to understand your future spouse's family traditions; if possible, incorporate some of them in your own life.

Constant communication is imperative. Try to explain your feelings and needs. You will need your spouse's full support. Play role-reversal. Hopefully you can agree on most things and grow together as a Jewish couple, but you may need to take the lead and set the pace. This is your chance to grow and learn together! Use the rabbi as a catalyst for talking out the personal issues.

How will my future spouse's family feel about me and my conversion?

All Jewish families are not the same. Each comes with its own individuals, interests, and values. Some families are observant and very knowledgeable about Judaism, others know much less and are less involved. If your future spouse's family is well informed and seriously committed, let them know how excited you are to have such a wonderful resource upon which to draw. Hopefully they will embrace you with open arms and help you to get more comfortable with Judaism and its many rituals.

If your partner's family does not know much about Judaism, it is possible that family members may feel a bit intimidated by you and your rapidly growing knowledge. In any event, you cannot expect to draw upon them very much as a personal learning resource. Begin slowly to share your new experiences with them. You may even find that you have rekindled some of their childhood Jewish memories.

In most cases it will take some time for your new in-laws to know you as a Jew. Be patient and loving, and always keep the communication lines open in order to better understand their feelings and to help them understand yours.

How will other Jews treat me?

Finding a place for yourself in the Jewish community is a process that begins before conversion and may continue for months and sometimes years afterward. Obviously reactions will differ. Some born Jews will find it easy to accept you and will see your decision to convert as an endorsement of Judaism and the Jewish way of life. Some will try to be accepting but nonetheless feel uncomfortable around converts. Some find it difficult to understand why anyone would want to convert to Judaism in the first place. (This is often the case with less knowledgeable Jews.)

Very often, born Jews are more tolerant of converts to Judaism if the convert's notion of what it means to be Jewish conforms to their view. In many cases converts who actively pursue Judaism are more likely to be accepted than passive ones. This is because you are exhibiting your willingness to learn and become educated, which is one of the key values in Judaism. Occasionally there may be guilt and ambivalence on the part of born Jews who feel threatened by a convert who knows more than they do and who is more enthusiastic about Judaism than they are.

It is important for you to seek your personal Jewish identity through your own individual methods and not through the opinions of others. Finding acceptance within your community may take time. Again, it is prudent to be patient. Jewish feelings must be nurtured if they are to develop. Time, determination, and practice will make you feel more Jewish. As a new Jew you may be intellectually and cognitively ready, but emotionally you may not yet be there. Sharing the feelings of a born Jew about issues like Israel or anti-Semitism or the Holocaust will take time and the experience of being with other Jews.

5
Raising Children in a Conversionary Marriage

And you shall teach them to your children . . .
                                    —*Deuteronomy 6:7*

What are some guidelines for raising children in a conversionary marriage?

Converts learn through and/or with their children as they become Jewishly educated. Your decision to become a Jew will have a significant effect on your children. There will undoubtedly be a variety of challenges, especially in the early months and years. You may wonder how you will ever be able to effectively pass Judaism on to your children when you yourself are still in the process of becoming comfortable with it. Many other questions, thoughts, and doubts may arise. How do you teach children to interact comfortably with their relatives when some are Jewish and some aren't?

When your children are infants, of course, they know nothing about your conversion and its background. As they grow older and become more aware of religious holidays and traditions, however, you will need to explain the difference between the two sets of grandparents and the other Jewish and non-Jewish relatives and their families. Make sure that your explanations are sensitive and on a level your child is capable of understanding. Remember that the child's own developing identity may be affected by what you say and how you say it.

Treating both sets of families with love and respect at all times sends a very important signal. Explain to your children that they can *share* religious holidays with their non-Jewish relatives, but not *celebrate* with them. Any questions they ask about the other religion ought to be dealt with maturely and not ignored.

Many converts feel it important for families to be together as often as possible, especially on nonreligious occasions, such as birthdays, anniversaries, and civic holidays like Thanksgiving and the Fourth of July. This togetherness helps to strengthen relationships and lines of communication.

Remember that the patterns of adjustment for converts and their relatives are quite varied, and different situations arise from family to family. For example, we have been talking until now about converts who do not have children, but some converts are also parents. In such cases, especially if the children are older, it is very important to work gradually and not introduce changes too quickly. Be aware, too, that children born of a non-Jewish mother before she converts are not considered Jewish, and if they are to become Jewish will need to go through a formal conversion process. For a male this means ritual circumcision, or the ritual of *hatafat dam brit* if he is already circumcised (see p. 33), and immersion in a mikvah. For a female, immersion in the mikvah is all that is necessary.

With patience, persistence, open communication, and true sensitivity to everyone's feelings, your family will come to respect your traditions, and your children will be the beneficiaries of a more loving relationship.

6

Your Emotions

Sing to God a new song.

—*Psalms 96:1*

What feelings can I expect to have during the stages of my conversion?

Anyone converting to Judaism has a large number of issues to consider, among them choosing a sponsoring rabbi, a conversion class, the branch of Judaism, and the impact of becoming a Jew on family, marriage, and friends. Once you make the initial decision to convert, you will probably feel a sense of relief and an enthusiastic desire to zealously move forward.

You will have many other kinds of feelings after you embark on the formal learning process. It is not possible to predict how you will feel or respond to issues along the way, but be prepared for a variety of intense emotions.

Some converts spend a lot of time thinking about their personal religious beliefs, their parents and families, and their past lives. Fear of the unknown and of feeling inferior to other Jews are common themes sounded by many prospective converts.

As the conversion process continues, it is quite common to feel totally overwhelmed by the huge amount of facts and information you have to learn. This can lead to feelings of anxiety and inadequacy.

Remember that becoming Jewish requires considerable time and your full, whole-hearted commitment. Take one step at a time. Don't be too hard on yourself, for conversion is a very big step in your life. Move on to another book or ritual only when you feel ready to do so. Do not set unrealistic goals for yourself. Be patient, and try not to become discouraged. Do not feel pressured, and do not let others pressure you into converting before you are ready.

As the completion of your program draws closer, you are likely to feel both relief and apprehension. Being anxious is perfectly normal, for it is no small matter to change your religious identity and affiliation.

What can I do to feel more Jewish?

Feeling more Jewish is a continuing challenge to prospective converts. A Jewish identity is something that you have to build. Although the road to building a Jewish identity begins with formal classroom learning, there are many other resources that can help you to feel more Jewish. You should be able to find many of them in the Jewish community at large.

Finding and developing a network of caring and knowledgeable Jewish friends can be very helpful. Supportive friendships will help you to become a part of your local Jewish community and provide a comfortable Jewish environment in which you can learn and ask questions.

Begin to use a Jewish calendar to measure time. (For details on the differences between the Jewish and secular calendars, see the appendix.) Note the Jewish holidays. When they occur, try to experience them through attendance at synagogue services and in a supportive Jewish home.

As you learn various prayers and rituals, practice using and reciting them. Lighting Shabbat and festival candles or saying the Kiddush blessing over wine are good starting points, once you learn how to do them. Everything will feel totally foreign at first—but repetition and time help to make things second nature. Set small, attainable goals for yourself; the things you learn will eventually become part of the fabric of your Jewish life.

For example, learn the blessing over bread (*hamotzi*) and say it at a regular weekday dinner. Learn one prayer at a time. On each holiday, learn or do one new thing: a prayer, a song, a recipe, a ritual, a story. Begin to establish your own traditions!

Buy books of Jewish interest and read them. Buy Jewish records. Watch and listen to television and radio programs of Jewish interest. Subscribe to Jewish magazines and weekly newspapers.

If you are fortunate enough to have a college or university B'nai B'rith Hillel Foundation in your area, seek out the Hillel rabbi and find out what kinds of Jewish programming are available to you.

If there is a Jewish museum in your community, it can be an extremely important resource. In addition to their permanent and temporary exhibits, many museums have outstanding Judaic gift shops. Some offer a broad spectrum of educational activities and classes as well.

A Jewish community center also affords many cultural and social opportunities. Finally, your local Jewish Federation will be able to provide you with information about all of the Jewish activities and institutions in your community. This might include the local synagogues and their adult and family programs as well as brotherhoods and sisterhoods, Hadassah, B'nai B'rith, ORT, and the National Council of Jewish Women. Giving of your time and energy to some of these will help you meet new friends and become more comfortable as a member of the Jewish community.

How will I feel on Jewish and Christian holidays?

Converts-to-be sometimes feel as if they are in a state of limbo—no longer really Christian, but not yet Jewish. Questions of belonging and what to call oneself are not uncommon. (These may even be a catalyst for "setting the date" for your conversion.) A prospective Jew may no longer have intellectual ties with his or her former faith but will still need much time before attaining the emotional readiness to feel inwardly Jewish. This unsettled feeling is especially apparent upon the onset of religious holidays, whether Christian or Jewish. Questions such as "Is it okay to celebrate one more Easter?" or "Is it okay to celebrate Passover, a holiday with which I am still relatively unfamiliar?" are quite common.

It is entirely unrealistic for you to expect to disengage yourself totally from the known and familiar, and suddenly thrust yourself into the celebration of Jewish holidays. Your entry into Jewish festival celebrations ought to be gradual, depending on your intellectual and emotional readiness. At the outset, when you have less knowledge and experience, you may choose to be an interested observer, and perhaps even an active participant-observer, of Jewish holidays, rituals, and customs. As you gain more knowledge through study and the passage of time, you will begin to experience Jewish holidays and practices personally by attempting to observe and carry out some of their rituals and traditions. Here is where Jewish friends and family can be invaluable in teaching you, encouraging you, and gently easing you into the world of Jewish observance. As time passes, your growing involvement in Jewish observances will help you feel connected to the Jewish people.

Can I spend Christian holidays with my family?

Converts and prospective converts are often confused about how to act with their parents and other non-Jewish relatives at holiday times. One of my students described her December dilemma in this way:

"December is the most difficult emotional time. Even for non-practicing Christians, Christmas is often the center of most family traditions, childhood memories, and good feelings. Emotionally, giving up Christmas as your holiday is very difficult. Converts have to let go of the emotion and childhood dreams. I know I can never share with my children the same experiences and traditions I loved as a child. I also feel guilty for denying my parents the joy and tradition of spoiling their future grandchildren at Christmas.

"Total and constant Christmas reminders around us are difficult. As a *new* Jew, you want to turn off the Christmas spirit around you, because you don't feel comfortable being just an observer.

"Time and self-reflection have helped me. I've realized I can *enjoy* what's going on around me during the Christmas season and still be a good Jew. The decorations are beautiful, the songs can be fun to listen to, and the feelings of love and goodwill and family togetherness are important to every religion. I'm learning how to be an observer, and I'm feeling more comfortable with my family. We spend Christmas together and I give them gifts. I'm still trying to have them stop giving me gifts at Christmas; instead, I'd prefer them at Hanukkah. They *love* Christmas, and it's hard for them to change. My sister has been really great and supportive. Because of the difficulty in letting go of Christmas traditions, I've started making a strong effort to create Jewish traditions in my home, the easiest being Hanukkah. With young stepchildren, it's easy to get excited. I've tried to make holidays happy, fun, and educational for them.

"Rituals and traditions are very comforting. They make you feel like you belong, and help to build new, happy memories. The pain of losing Christmas is not as deep."

Prospective converts often have to grapple with such questions as the propriety of attending a family Christmas dinner or Easter get-together. Here again, there are no simple rules of thumb that will work for all converts and their families.

Some converts find it perfectly acceptable to visit their families at Christian holiday time and join them for dinner. They do this with the mutual understanding that they are joining their family as *they* celebrate *their* holiday. Other converts insist on inviting their families to celebrate Jewish holidays with them in their own homes. One of my students says that doing this "is a great way to make *your* family a part of your new life."

Another expressed this feeling:

"One of my most memorable experiences with respect to celebrating a Jewish holiday took place when I prepared Passover dinner for my fiancee's family. We all sat around the table and read from the Haggadah. Our Seder plate, food, and wine were prepared in the traditional way. Most important of all, *I* prepared it. The family was very impressed and enjoyed the holiday as celebrated by the traditions my fiancee and I created."

Remember that it will take time for you to "unlearn" a holiday celebration that was once an integral part of your life. You will need time to be fully comfortable with Jewish holidays and their traditions. It will take time for your family to get used to your observing them. Converts often feel it is important to be together with their own families as much as possible for nonreligious occasions, such as birthdays or anniversaries, or civic holidays such as Thanksgiving or the Fourth of July. These are times when families can be truly united in a pleasant and easy-going setting of friendship and togetherness, without the constant tension of a "my holiday/ your holiday" syndrome.

With the passage of time and continued open dialogue, religious holiday sharing with your non-Jewish family ought to become less awkward, with decreased anxiety and increased cordiality.

The Day of Your Conversion

This is the day that God has made; let us exult and rejoice on it.

—*Psalms 118:24*

*H*ow am I likely to feel on the day of my conversion?

The day of one's conversion is generally very exciting and emotional. Some converts have mixed reactions combining apprehension about the future with relief that the program has finally ended and reaching the goal is in sight. Although feelings of anxiety are normal, it is important to remember that the members of the Bet Din (Jewish religious court) who will ask you the questions are trying to determine your readiness, knowing full well that your sponsoring rabbi would not have convened them unless he or she felt that you were emotionally and intellectually ready. It may be helpful for you to speak to other converts to find out what their experiences were like on their conversion days.

One of my students had this to say:

"For me, it started out as anxious, nervous excitement. I couldn't sleep the night before. I kept concentrating on academics, like it was a really important 'final exam.' Driving to the temple, I was happy—and scared. I knew I wanted to convert, but I'd never made such a serious decision about my life. For me, choosing Judaism was a personal decision of how I wanted to worship God and live my life—not just a step necessary before getting married.

"For me, the questioning of the Bet Din was very satisfying—but I was so nervous! I knew I did well and was excited about the mikvah.

"While I was immersing and reciting the blessings, I was really concentrating on doing it correctly. After coming out of the water, I didn't experience any 'rush of spirituality.' Getting dressed I felt extremely happy and relieved. I kept looking in the mirror to see if I looked any different—and kept saying 'I'm really Jewish now.' I felt strange—like I was outside my body watching the events.

"When I joined everyone again I read a declaration of faith in which I declared my desire to accept the principles of Judaism and follow its practices. When I received my Hebrew name, the emotion really hit me. Rich was fighting back the tears, and I just couldn't stop smiling. In the hours following, I felt so happy and relieved. I could finally say that 'I'm Jewish.' I experienced a feeling of peace and contentment, like I've never known before. I had a strange, strong feeling that God was looking at me and smiling. It was the happiest day of my life—equivalent to my wedding day!"

Your experience at the mikvah and with the Bet Din should be comfortable and meaningful, providing you with a positive entry into your new life as a Jew.

What is a Bet Din? What types of questions will I be asked?

When your sponsoring rabbi is satisfied that you have acquired a basic knowledge of Judaism and are sincere about living a Jewish life, the final step leading to your conversion will be taken. Arrangements will be made to go before a Bet Din, a Jewish court of three rabbis. This court will often convene at a place where there is a Jewish ritual bath called a mikvah. In this way the entire process of conversion can occur on the same day. However, the meeting with the Bet Din and immersion in the mikvah do not necessarily have to take place on the same day.

All male candidates must be ritually circumcised before immersing in the mikvah. If a male has already been circumcised medically, the ritual must be completed through *hatafat dam brit.* In this ceremony a drop of blood is painlessly drawn from the tip of the penis to complete the requirement for entrance into the covenant.

The members of the Bet Din (one of whom is usually your sponsoring rabbi) will begin their deliberations by asking about your background. Sample questions might include: In what religion were you raised? Were you ever devoutly religious? What is your family like? When did you first entertain the idea of becoming a Jew?

The next set of questions is generally meant to determine your knowledge of Judaism as well as your appreciation for rituals and other aspects of the Jewish religion. The answers to these questions will help the Bet Din to evaluate your Judaic cognitive knowledge as well as your emotional attachment to Judaism. Sample questions here might include: What is the Havdalah ceremony, and what are the elements of its ritual? Why do we light two Shabbat candles? Why is it customary to eat matzah on Passover? What are the themes of the Rosh HaShanah liturgy? What are some of the elements of a Passover Seder?

Sample opinion questions might include: What is your favorite Jewish holiday and why? Who is your most likable Bible personality? What prayer do you most enjoy?

The third category of questions is geared to determining whether the candidate is prepared to fulfill the commandments of Judaism and abide by its laws. Some examples are: Do you freely choose, without any reservations, to enter the eternal covenant between God and the Jewish people, thereby becoming a Jew of your own free will? Do you accept Judaism to the exclusion of all other religious faiths, doctrines, practices, and affiliations? If you should be blessed with children, do you promise to rear them as Jews? As a non-Jew, you have the option of observing Jewish law, such as kashrut or the Shabbat, if you wish, and of not observing it if you prefer; either choice is acceptable. Once you convert to Judaism, however, Jewish law becomes obligatory for you, just as it is for every other Jew. Do you understand this? Do you have any problem or reservation about this?

After the period of questioning, the Bet Din will ask you to leave the room while they discuss your answers and the interview. Once it is determined that you have successfully completed the test and interview, you will be qualified for immersion in a mikvah.

What is a mikvah? What blessings and other ritual acts will I need to know?

A mikvah (lit. "gathering of water") is a Jewish ritual bath. For many centuries, every Jewish community has maintained a mikvah for the use of its members. The water in a mikvah must come from a natural spring or river; the mikvah itself must be a minimum of two feet square by six feet high, and must be filled with close to two hundred gallons of water, an amount sufficient for average-sized persons to immerse themselves. Immersion in a mikvah is required by traditional Jewish law for the purpose of ritual purification and cleanliness of the body.

In order for your immersion to be valid, it is necessary that the mikvah water come into contact with all parts of your body. Before immersing yourself, you must be cleansed. A bathtub or shower in the mikvah area will always be available for this purpose. When you enter the mikvah you must be totally unclothed, with all jewelry removed. A covering will be draped over you, which the mikvah attendant (male or female, as appropriate) will remove as you descend the steps into the mikvah. (The members of the Bet Din wait outside the door that leads into the mikvah in order to hear that you recite the blessings properly.)

Standing with your legs apart and arms hanging lose, bend over and immerse yourself completely so that every part of your body, including your hair, is touched by the water. Then, standing erect, recite this blessing:

Barukh atah adonai eloheinu melekh ha-olam, asher kid'shanu b'mitzvotav v'tzivanu al ha-tevilah.

Praised are You, Eternal our God, Sovereign of the Universe whose mitzvot add holiness to our lives, and who gave us the mitzvah of immersion.

Next, immerse yourself completely two more times and recite this blessing:

Barukh atah adonai eloheinu melekh ha-olam, sheh-heh-heh-ya-nu v'keey'manu v'hee-gee-anu lazman hazeh.

Praised are You, Eternal our God, Sovereign of the Universe, for granting us life, for sustaining us, and for helping us to reach this day.

Once you have completed the immersion and the blessings, you will remove yourself from the mikvah and get fully dressed. A short ceremony now follows during which the conversion document is signed by the members of the Bet Din. Some sponsoring rabbis will also have you recite a Declaration of Faith and *Shema Yisrael*. This is generally followed by a prayer conferring a Hebrew name upon you. Following the naming is a *mi shebayrach* prayer asking God to bless you and enable you to prosper in all of your endeavors.

Who and what should I bring to the mikvah?

The mikvah will generally provide you with towels. Some will also provide a hairdryer. Many candidates bring a camera in order to photograph the signing of the conversion document by the Bet Din and to take a picture with their sponsoring rabbi. You may also want to invite some guests—your future spouse, his or her family, your own family, a close friend or recent convert who can give you any needed emotional support. Please remember that your guests will not be allowed in the room where the questioning takes place, but a close friend or family member of the same sex is generally allowed to go into the mikvah area with you.

Very often, converts and their guests eat lunch or dinner together after the conversion ceremony.

How do I choose a Hebrew name?

Male born Jews are given their Hebrew names immediately following the ritual circumcision, which takes place eight days after birth. Female born Jews are often named in the synagogue, soon after birth, on a day when there is a reading from the Torah. Namings for girls also take place in the home. There are several designations for the naming-a-girl ceremony, among them *Simḥat Bat* and *Zeved HaBat*.

The Hebrew name used when someone participates in a Jewish ritual comprises his or her own name followed by the Hebrew word *ben* ("son of") or *bat* ("daughter of"), the father's name, and often the mother's name. A man, for example, might be named Reuven ben Yaakov v'Sarah (Reuben the son of Jacob and Sarah) and a woman, Miryam bat Avraham v'Rachel (Miriam the daughter of Abraham and Rachel).

Converts to Judaism are customarily referred to as the son or daughter of Abraham and Sarah, the first Jewish patriarch and matriarch. You may choose any first name you wish. In some instances you may be able to find an exact Hebrew equivalent of your English first name. Some female candidates choose the first name Ruth, since she was such a prominent and beloved convert in Jewish history. For a complete list of Hebrew names, see the books listed in the appendix.

8

Leading a Jewish Life

These words which I command you this day you shall take to heart.

—Deuteronomy 6:6

What happens after my conversion?

Many converts report a feeling of letdown in the initial weeks after the conversion ceremony. Beforehand, they had imagined that the ceremony would end the process of becoming a Jew, but they found that it was really just the beginning. For some new converts, the transition to making their own way through the Jewish community is difficult. Once your conversion is formalized, you will have to work diligently in order to find your own personal niche in the Jewish community. Forming your own individual Jewish identity and set of Jewish values, and finding a comfortable group of friends with whom to integrate, are among the challenges. Your spouse, your sponsoring rabbi, and your family will continue to work with you and provide the support, information, and opportunities for a variety of religious, cultural, and social experiences in a pleasant, positive, and nonthreatening environment. All of your role models can play a very important part in easing your entry into the Jewish communal world.

Synagogue affiliation is a must and will provide you with an important port of entry into the Jewish community. Attending services and participating in synagogue programs, including adult education classes, is highly recommended.

You may also look for fulfillment in Jewish organizations dedicated to social action or Jewish culture. Jews by choice often report that the more active they were in such organizations, the more comfortable they felt in the Jewish community and the more accepted they were by the community.

Remember to be patient with yourself. It takes time to feel totally comfortable with your Jewishness, especially if you are also adapting to a new life as a married person.

How do I begin living a Jewish life?

The time of conversion is the best time to officially declare your desire to accept the principles of Judaism and to follow its ceremonies and practices. Since Judaism is primarily a home-focused way of life, you will want to work together with your spouse. Remember that the two of you may not always be ready for the same things at the same time when living a Jewish life. Keep communicating and experimenting!

Each holiday celebration, with its home symbols, foods, rituals, music, and tales, can bring delight to you and beauty and joy to living as a Jew.

The Jewish home is often referred to as a *mikdash me'at*, a miniature sanctuary. A sanctuary is marked by tranquility and holiness. The kind of sanctuary you build together with your family will depend on the choices you make.

As you begin your life as a Jew, try to see each new day as an opportunity to practice your Judaism. Continue to study and increase your repertoire of knowledge and of fulfillment of mitzvot. Practice the mitzvot with joy! Make prayer a regular part of your life. Practice your Hebrew skills. Discover the happiness of celebrating Jewish holidays throughout the year. Because Shabbat comes every week, try to make it an opportunity for personal re-creation. Begin to collect ritual items, such as a Kiddush cup, Shabbat candlesticks, a Havdalah set, a Hanukkiah, a Passover Seder plate, and a matzah cover. Affix mezuzot to the doors of your house or apartment. Continue to stock your personal library with Jewish books and magazines.

Remember not to focus only on religious ritual. Judaism is also a culture. It includes Jewish museums, dance, art, literature, theatre, and drama. Try to visit places of Jewish interest as often as you can, including a trip to Israel, if at all possible. Finally, make every effort to offer your time and energy to communal organizations that need your assistance, including synagogues, homes for the aged, food banks, and the like. Extending your concern to others through specific activities is an important Jewish value. By making a lifelong commitment to live and learn as a Jew, you will surely come to know the richness and beauty of our heritage.

On the following pages you will find a summary of some basic Jewish information to help you along the way, including a glossary and a suggested reading list. We hope that it will help you to bring into your home the values, customs, and traditions that have enabled the Jewish family and the Jewish people to endure.

Appendix

The Jewish Calendar

Unlike the secular (Gregorian) calendar, which is solar, the Jewish calendar is both lunar and solar. The months are fixed by the moon's movements around the earth, the years by the earth's revolution around the sun. Originally the Jewish calendar was purely lunar, with the year ending after twelve months had elapsed, but since lunar months are shorter than solar months, the seasons soon began to "move." Spring, for instance, occurred a few days earlier every year. As a result, the Jewish holidays often did not fall in the seasons specified in the Bible. To prevent this problem, a system of coordinating the lunar year with the solar year had to be devised. The method adopted utilizes the periodic addition of a "leap month" to make the two years equal in length.

In biblical times, the first month of the Hebrew calendar was Nisan. It was on the fifteenth of Nisan, now commemorated as the first day of Passover, that the Israelites achieved freedom from Egyptian slavery. The return from the Babylonian Exile, however, occurred in the fall, and that is why Rosh HaShanah, the New Year festival, is celebrated on the first day of the autumn month of Tishri.

There are twelve months in the Hebrew calendar. Based on the moon's cycle around the earth, each of them has either 29 or 30 days, and thus the lunar year is 354 days long. In contrast, a solar year is 365 days. To make up the difference, and keep the lunar year coordinated with the solar cycle, an extra month is added to the Jewish year approximately once every three years.

Here are the names of the months of the Hebrew calendar:

1. Nisan (ניסן)
2. Iyar (אייר)
3. Sivan (סיון)
4. Tammuz (תמוז)
5. Av (אב)

6. Elul (אלול)
7. Tishri (תשרי)
8. Ḥeshvan (חשון)
9. Kislev (כסלו)
10. Tevet (טבת)

11. Shevat (שבט)
12. Adar (אדר)
13. Adar II (אדר ב') [only in a leap year]

The Jewish calendar numbers the years from the date of the world's creation as determined by Jewish tradition. The book you are now reading was first published in 5753 (1992-93); in other words, 5,753 years after the beginning of the world—or symbolically, since the beginning of consciously recorded time. The secular calendar, in contrast, counts years from the birth of Jesus, using the abbreviation A.D. (*anno domini*, meaning "in the year of our Lord"). Dates before the birth of Jesus are followed by the abbreviation B.C. ("before Christ"). Thus A.D. 1993 means 1,993 years after the birth of Jesus.

For Jews and others sensitive to Jewish tradition, it is customary when citing dates in the civil calendar to use the abbreviation C.E. ("common era") instead of A.D., and B.C.E. ("before the common era") instead of B.C.

Our Jewish Holidays

A Brief Summary

SHABBAT (Sabbath)

Date
Seventh day of every week.

Duration
One day (from sundown on Friday until approximately twenty-five hours later on Saturday night).

Name of holiday
Day of Rest (*Yom Menuḥah*).

Source
And God blessed the seventh day and declared it holy, because on it God ceased from all the work of creation.
—*Genesis 2:3*

General Theme
The Sabbath, the holiest day in the week, commemorates the creation of the world. It is a day devoted to prayer, study, rest, relaxation, spirituality, and enjoyment. The Sabbath is our weekly reminder that God rested from work of creation. Of all the holidays in the Torah, only the Sabbath is mentioned in the Ten Commandments (Exodus 20:8). We are commanded to observe and remember the Sabbath, and to keep it holy.

Personal Theme
An opportunity to cease from daily work, proclaiming God as

Sovereign of the world and allowing ourselves to be rejuvenated.

Traditional Foods
Braided loaves of bread (*ḥallot*), gefilte fish, wine, chicken.

Customs
1. Preparations for the Sabbath include house cleaning, personal
    cleanliness and wearing our best clothing, and dropping some
    coins into a *tzedakah* (charity) box before candlelighting on
    Friday.

2. Two candles are lit just before sunset, and the appropriate
    blessing is recited (see p. 80).

3. The Friday evening Sabbath service takes place in the synagogue.
    The traditional greeting on the Sabbath is *Shabbat Shalom*
    ("Sabbath Peace"). Following services is an Oneg Shabbat at
    which refreshments and beverages are served, offering an
    opportunity for socializing and sometimes for study and discus-
    sion.

4. It is customary for parents to bless their children before sitting
    down to the Sabbath meal (see p. 80). The blessing for boys
    invokes the examples of Jacob's grandchildren Ephraim and
    Manasseh who, although raised in Egypt, did not lose their
    identity as Jews. The blessing for girls recalls the four matriarchs,
    Sarah, Rebekah, Rachel, and Leah.

5. The Friday evening meal begins with the Kiddush blessing over
    wine (see p. 81). This is followed by the ritual washing of the
    hands and the Hamotzi benediction over two *ḥallot*, which recall
    the double portion of manna God provided for the Israelites (see
    p. 82-83).

6. The Shabbat meal should be served at a relaxed pace. Many
    families sing Shabbat songs (*zemirot*) between the courses.

7. The meal concludes with the blessings after the meal (*Birkat*

Hamazon) (see p. 84).

8. At the service on Saturday morning a *sidrah* (selection) from the Torah is read, followed by a prophetic portion known as a *Haftarah*.

9. Shabbat afternoon is a time for a variety of experiences that change the usually hectic pace of daily life. Taking a nap, reading, studying, and visiting local friends all provide a relaxing shift from weekday pressures.

10. On Shabbat afternoon the Minḥah service introduces the Torah portion to be read the following Saturday morning. This is followed by the third Shabbat meal (*seudah sh'li-sheet*), usually a simple dairy meal, customarily accompanied by the singing of Shabbat songs.

11. The Saturday evening service concludes with the Havdalah (separation) ceremony (see p.87). The ceremonial objects used for Havdalah are a Kiddush cup filled with wine (wine sanctifies reentry into the secular world), a spice box (spices suggest that the memory of the Shabbat just gone by will linger and be fragrant), and a braided multi-wick candle (fire reminds us that light was the first of God's creations after the completion of the heavens and the earth).

ROSH HASHANAH (New Year)

Date
First two days of Tishri.

Duration
Two days for Conservative, Reconstructionist, and Orthodox Jews and for Jews in Israel. One day for Reform Jews.

Names of Holiday
1. Day of Blowing the Shofar (*Yom Teruah*).
2. Day of Remembrance (*Yom HaZikaron*).

3. Day of Judgment (*Yom HaDin*).

Source
In the seventh month, on the first day of the month, you shall observe
complete rest, a sacred occasion commemorated with loud blasts.
—*Leviticus 23:24*

General Theme
Rosh HaShanah is the beginning of a solemn ten-day period, known
as the Days of Awe (*Yamim Noraim*), that concludes on Yom Kippur.
     As the new year begins, God judges people for the coming year.
In order to judge us fairly, God remembers and weighs all of our acts
in the past year before giving a final verdict. Rosh HaShanah also
commemorates the birthday of the world.

Personal Theme
The personal theme of Rosh HaShanah is renewal. In admitting our
mistakes, we ask for forgiveness. It is a time for self-examination, new
resolutions, and earnest efforts to correct our faults.

Foods
1. Round *hallah*, suggesting a crown and thereby symbolizing
    God's sovereignty.

2. Apples dipped in honey, symbolizing the wish for a sweet and
    fruitful year.

3. Honey cake and *taiglakh* (honey pastry).

Customs
1. Festival candles are lit in the home at sunset. The following
    blessing is recited:

בָּרוּךְ אַתָּה יהוה אֱלֹהֵינוּ מֶלֶךְ הָעוֹלָם, אֲשֶׁר קִדְּשָׁנוּ בְּמִצְוֹתָיו,
וְצִוָּנוּ לְהַדְלִיק נֵר שֶׁל (שַׁבָּת וְשֶׁל) יוֹם טוֹב.

*Barukh atah adonai eloheinu melekh ha-olam, asher kid'shanu
b'mitzvotav v'tzivanu lehadlik ner shel (Shabbat v'shel) Yom Tov.*

Praised are You, Eternal our God, Sovereign of the Universe whose mitzvot add holiness to our lives, and who gave us the mitzvah to kindle light for (Shabbat and for) the festival.

2. The Kiddush (blessing over wine) for Rosh HaShanah is recited before the evening meal. This is followed by *Sheh-heh-heh-yanu*, the prayer of gratitude for reached this season. *Sheh-heh-heh-yanu* is recited at the start of all festivals and also is often said when eating a new fruit for the first time in a season.

בָּרוּךְ אַתָּה יהוה אֱלֹהֵינוּ מֶלֶךְ הָעוֹלָם, שֶׁהֶחֱיָנוּ וְקִיְּמָנוּ וְהִגִּיעָנוּ לַזְּמַן הַזֶּה.

Barukh atah adonai eloheinu melekh ha-olam, sheh-heh-heh-yanu v'keey'manu v'hee-gee-anu lazman hazeh.

Praised are you, Eternal our God, Sovereign of the Universe, for granting us life, for sustaining us, and for helping us to reach this day.

3. Apples are dipped in honey, symbolizing the hope that sweetness will enter the lives of all Jews in the coming year. The following petition is recited:

יְהִי רָצוֹן מִלְּפָנֶיךָ, יהוה אֱלֹהֵינוּ וֵאלֹהֵי אֲבוֹתֵינוּ, שֶׁתְּחַדֵּשׁ עָלֵינוּ שָׁנָה טוֹבָה וּמְתוּקָה.

Yehi ratzon milfanekha adonai eloheinu velohei avoteinu she'tehadesh aleinu shanah tovah u'metukah.

May it be your desire, Eternal our God and God of our ancestors, to renew for us a sweet and good year.

4. *Hamotzi* (blessing over the bread) is recited over a round *hallah* (usually in the shape of a king's crown) symbolizing God's sovereignty.

בָּרוּךְ אַתָּה יהוה אֱלֹהֵינוּ מֶלֶךְ הָעוֹלָם, הַמּוֹצִיא לֶחֶם מִן הָאָרֶץ.

Barukh atah adonai eloheinu melekh ha-olam, ha-motzi lehem min ha-aretz

Praised are You, Eternal our God, Sovereign of the Universe who brings forth bread from the earth.

5. During synagogue services, the rabbi and the cantor (and congregants who follow this custom) wear a white robe (*kittel*). The color white, symbolizing purity and renewal, is reminiscent of the following words read in the Rosh HaShanah service: "Though your sins be as scarlet, they shall become as white as snow" (Isaiah 1:18). It is also customary to replace the colored ark curtain, the Torah mantles, and the cover on the reader's table with white ones.

6. When greeting people, it is customary to use the phrase *L'shanah tovah tikatevu,* meaning "May you be inscribed for a good year." This phrase also appears on Rosh Ha-Shanah greeting cards which are often sent to friends and family. Other traditional greetings include *Shanah tovah* ("Have a good year") and *Ketivah v'ḥatimah tovah* ("May you be inscribed and sealed for a good year").

7. The shofar (ram's horn) is sounded during services (except when Rosh HaShanah falls on a Sabbath), with the goal of awakening us to repentance.

8. On the first day of Rosh HaShanah in the afternoon (or on the second day in the afternoon if the first day is a Sabbath) Jews customarily gather at a nearby stream or river to symbolically cast away their sins. This ceremony is called Tashlikh (lit. "to cast off"), and includes the verse from the Book of Micah (7:19), "And You will cast (*v'tashlikh*) all their sins into the depths of the sea."

9. It is customary to visit the graves of departed family members before Rosh HaShanah, during the month of Elul.

YOM KIPPUR (Day of Atonement)

Date
Tenth of Tishri.

Duration
One day for Jews of all denominations and in all places.

Name of Holiday
Sabbath of Sabbaths (*Shabbat Shabbaton*).

Source
Mark, the tenth day of this seventh month is the Day of Atonement. It shall be a sacred occasion for you: you shall practice self-denial . . . .
—*Leviticus 23:27*

General Theme
Yom Kippur concludes the solemn ten-day period of the Yamim Noraim that begins on Rosh HaShanah. We abstain from eating and drinking, confess our sins, and ask for forgiveness, praying that we will be sealed in God's Book of Life. We all feel responsible for one another.

Personal Theme
Atonement, integrity, renewal, and a desire that our fast will lead us to help others in distress.

Customs
1. We participate in a festive meal before sunset on the eve of Yom Kippur.

2. The holiday is ushered in by lighting two candles and reciting the following:

בָּרוּךְ אַתָּה יהוה אֱלֹהֵינוּ מֶלֶךְ הָעוֹלָם, אֲשֶׁר קִדְּשָׁנוּ בְּמִצְוֹתָיו,
וְצִוָּנוּ לְהַדְלִיק נֵר שֶׁל (שַׁבָּת וְשֶׁל) יוֹם הַכִּפּוּרִים.

*Barukh atah adonai eloheinu melekh ha-olam, asher kid'shanu
b'mitzvotav v'tzivanu lehadlik ner shel (shabbat v'shel) Yom Ha-
kippurim.*

Praised are You, Eternal our God, Sovereign of the Universe
whose mitzvot add holiness to our lives, and who gave us the
mitzvah to kindle light for (Shabbat and for) Yom Kippur.

This is followed by the recitation of *Sheh-heh-heh-yanu.*

בָּרוּךְ אַתָּה יהוה אֱלֹהֵינוּ מֶלֶךְ הָעוֹלָם, שֶׁהֶחֱיָנוּ וְקִיְּמָנוּ וְהִגִּיעָנוּ
לַזְּמַן הַזֶּה.

*Barukh atah adonai eloheinu melekh ha-olam, sheh-heh-heh-
yanu v'keey' manu v'hee-gee-anu lazman hazeh.*

Praised are You, Eternal our God, Sovereign of the Universe, for
granting us life, for sustaining us, and for helping us to reach this
day.

3. Just before leaving for services, it is customary to light a yahrzeit
    candle as a memorial to the deceased members of the family.

4. As on Rosh HaShanah, the rabbi, cantor, and any congregants
    who follow the custom wear a white gown called *kittel.*

5. At Kol Nidrei, the evening Yom Kippur service, the *tallit* (prayer
    shawl) is worn. The *tallit* is normally only worn at morning
    services; its use at Kol Nidrei reflects an added dimension of piety
    appropriate to the solemnity of the occasion. The Kol Nidrei
    prayer, from which the service for Yom Kippur night takes its
    name, is recited while there is still daylight (when a *tallit* is worn),
    since it deals with the annulment of vows, a religio-legal
    procedure that must take place during the day and cannot take
    place on a Sabbath or on a festival.

6. The abstinence on Yom Kippur includes total fasting (no food or
    drink) for adults (except the sick or weak), abstaining from sexual

relations and bathing, and not using leather shoes (out of compassion for animals) or cosmetics.

7. The Yizkor memorial service is part of the morning service.

8. On Yom Kippur afternoon, at the Minḥah service, the entire Book of Jonah is chanted, reminding us that God's forgiveness is universal.

9. At the end of the Yom Kippur service a long blast of the shofar is sounded and the words *L'shanah ha-ba'ah bi-yerushalayim* ("Next year in Jerusalem") are proclaimed.

10. The greeting at the end of Yom Kippur is *G'mar ḥatimah tovah*, "May you be sealed (in the Book of Life) for a good verdict."

SUKKOT (Tabernacles; Booths)

Date
Begins on the fifteenth of Tishri.

Duration
Eight days for Conservative, Reconstructionist, and Orthodox Jews. Seven days for Reform Jews and Jews in Israel.

Names of Holiday
1. Festival of Ingathering (*Ḥag He-asif*).
2. *The* Festival (He-ḥag).
3. Day of Rejoicing (*Zeman Simḥateinu*).
4. Harvest Festival (*Ḥag Ha-katzir*).

Source
On the fifteenth of the seventh month there shall be a Feast of Booths to God, (to last) seven days. On the first day you shall take the produce of *hadar* trees, branches of palm trees, boughs of leafy trees, and willows of the brook, and you shall rejoice before God seven days. You shall live in booths seven days.
—*Leviticus* 23:34, 40, 42

General Theme

Sukkot marks the end of the fall harvest season, when the Israelites brought their first fruits to the Temple as a sign of thanksgiving for God's kindness. It also commemorates the Israelites' forty years of wandering in the desert. Since they built fragile huts to protect themselves from the elements, we are commanded to spend time in similar structures on Sukkot as a way of reminding ourselves of the fragility of life.

The Bible commands us to use the "four species" on Sukkot. These consist of the *etrog* (citron), the *lulav* (palm branch), and attached to the *lulav*, two sets of leaves—*hadassim* (myrtles, which are short and round) and *aravot* (willows, long and narrow). Various explanations have been given for the four species, including one in which the *etrog* represents the heart, the *lulav* the spine, the myrtle the eyes, and the willow the lips and mouth. According to this interpretation, the four species indicate that we are to serve God with every fiber of our being.

Personal Theme

Sukkot is a thanksgiving festival with many similarities to the American holiday of Thanksgiving.

Traditional Foods

1. Stuffed cabbage and *kreplach* (fried pockets of dough) containing fruit, fall harvest vegetables, or meat.

2. Dishes made with honey, such as *tsimmes* (prunes and other fruit, carrots, and honey) and *taiglakh* (honey pastry).

Customs

1. The holiday is ushered in with the lighting of at least two candles and the recitation of this blessing:

בָּרוּךְ אַתָּה יהוה אֱלֹהֵינוּ מֶלֶךְ הָעוֹלָם, אֲשֶׁר קִדְּשָׁנוּ בְּמִצְוֹתָיו,
וְצִוָּנוּ לְהַדְלִיק נֵר שֶׁל (שַׁבָּת וְשֶׁל) יוֹם טוֹב.

Barukh atah adonai eloheinu melekh ha-olam, asher kid'shanu
b'mitzvotav v'tzivanu lehadlik ner shel (Shabbat v'shel) Yom Tov.

Praised are You, Eternal our God, Sovereign of the Universe whose mitzvot add holiness to our lives, and who gave us the mitzvah to kindle light for (Shabbat and for) the festival.

2. The festival blessing over wine (Kiddush) is chanted in the *sukkah* (the "booth," or hut, erected for the holiday), followed by the *Sheh-heh-heh-yanu* blessing and the special blessing for dwelling in the *sukkah*. The latter blessing is:

בָּרוּךְ אַתָּה יהוה אֱלֹהֵינוּ מֶלֶךְ הָעוֹלָם, אֲשֶׁר קִדְּשָׁנוּ בְּמִצְוֹתָיו, וְצִוָּנוּ לֵשֵׁב בַּסֻּכָּה.

Barukh atah adonai eloheinu melekh ha-olam, asher kidshanu bemitzvotav vetzivanu layshev basukkah.

Praised are You, Eternal our God, Sovereign of the Universe whose mitzvot add holiness to our lives, and who gave us the mitzvah to dwell in the *sukkah*.

3. By tradition, the walls of the *sukkah* are decorated with posters bearing the names of seven special guests (*ushpizin*) whom we invite to be with us in the *sukkah* each day: Abraham, Isaac, Jacob, Joseph, Moses, Aaron, and David.

4. During the chanting of Hallel at Sukkot morning services, the *lulav* and *etrog* are waved in a prescribed pattern of movements. Hallel psalms recall the celebration of festivals in the ancient Temple and express our gratitude for God's protection and deliverance. (Note: The *lulav* and *etrog* are not used when Sukkot falls on a Sabbath.)

5. The *lulav* and *etrog* are carried in a procession during morning services. The Hoshanot prayers for redemption are recited as these *hakafot* (circuits) take place.

6. Meals are customarily served in the *sukkah* throughout the festival.

7. The seventh day of Sukkot is called Hoshanah Rabbah ("The Great Help") because of the special Hoshanah prayers of redemption recited on this day. On Hoshanah Rabbah the cantor dons a white gown (*kittel*). Our sages suggest that on this day God's judgment, sealed on Yom Kippur, receives final confirmation. Seven circuits (*hakafot*) are made around the sanctuary with the Torah carrier in the lead, followed by worshippers bearing *lulavim* and *etrogim*. Toward the end of the service, each worshipper takes a specially prepared bunch of willow leaves (called *hoshanot*) and strikes it against a chair or table. Just as a tree, after losing its leaves, renews its life through rain and warmth, so we can gain fresh strength for life's struggles and cares by renewed faith in God. The separation of the leaves from the twigs also symbolizes the separation of sin from our lives.

8. When one of the intermediate days of Sukkot falls on a Sabbath, the biblical Book of Ecclesiastes (*Kohelet*) is read before the Torah reading.

9. The greeting during Sukkot is *Ḥag samei'aḥ* ("Happy holiday") or *Mo'adim lesimḥah* ("May your festival be happy").

SHEMINI ATZERET AND SIMḤAT TORAH

Date
Twenty-second and twenty-third of Tishri.

Duration
Two days for Conservative, Reconstructionist, and Orthodox Jews. One day for Reform Jews and Jews living in Israel.

Source
On the eighth day you shall observe a sacred occasion ... it is a solemn gathering: you shall not work at your occupations.
—*Leviticus* 23:36

General Theme
These two days are attached to the end of the festival of Sukkot. Since Sukkot was one of the three Pilgrimage Festivals, the people extended their festivities and lingered in Jerusalem; thus the added eighth day of Shemini Atzeret. On Simḥat Torah (the ninth day), the reading from the Book of Deuteronomy concludes the yearly cycle of Torah readings, which immediately is begun anew with the reading of the first verses of Genesis.

Personal Theme
A new beginning in anticipation of an improved and better new year.

Customs
1. Two candles are lit to usher in both Shemini Atzeret and Simḥat Torah and the festival blessing is chanted (see p. 94). A yahrzeit candle is lit in memory of the departed.

2. Kiddush and Hamotzi are recited (see pp. 93 and 47).

3. On Shemini Atzeret, Yizkor memorial prayers for the departed are recited. At this time of year the rainy season is due to begin in Israel, where the crops depend heavily on an abundant rainfall, so the solemn prayer for rain (*Tefillat Geshem*) is added to the Musaf service. In most synagogues the cantor is attired in a white gown (*kittel*) because of the importance of the prayer for rain.

4. On Simhat Torah there is unrestricted merriment in the synagogue. People sing and dance while marching with the Torah scrolls. Children often carry banners and flags topped with apples. During the service a very special honor is awarded to two members of the congregation. The one given an *aliyah* to the Torah before the reading of the concluding passage of the Torah is referred to as the bridegroom of the Torah (*ḥatan Torah*), and the one given an *aliyah* to the Torah before the reading of the opening passages of Genesis is called the bridegroom of Genesis (*ḥatan Bereshit*). In addition, it is customary to call every adult member of the congregation to the Torah for an *aliyah*. Sometimes adults are called up collectively to say the Torah blessings,

standing under a large prayer shawl (*tallit*). Children are also given the opportunity to recite the blessings over the Torah, all standing together under a prayer shawl.

ḤANUKKAH

Date
Begins on the twenty-fifth of Kislev.

Duration
Eight days.

Name
Festival of Lights (*Ḥag Ha-urim*).

Source
They purified the Temple, removed the stones which defiled it. . . . they took unhewed stones, as the law commands, and built a new altar on the model of the old one. They rebuilt the Sanctuary and restored its interior and courts. They fixed the sacred vessels and menorah. When they had the shewbread on the table and had hung the curtains, and all their work was complete, then early on the twenty-fifth day of the month of Kislev. . . it was rededicated with hymns of thanksgiving. . . . Then Judah, his brothers, and the whole congregation of Israel decreed that the rededication of the altar should be observed with joy and gladness at the same time each year.
—*I Maccabees* 4:39-59

General Theme
Ḥanukkah marks the first time in recorded history that a war was fought in order to win freedom of religion. About twenty-one hundred years ago, Antiochus, a Syrian tyrant, set out to destroy the Jewish religion and replace it with Greek idol worship. He suffered a stunning defeat by the Maccabees, who not only defeated the enemy but recaptured and rededicated the Jerusalem Temple. There was only one small cruse of pure oil left when they entered the Temple, but

through a miracle it burned for eight days. That is why candles are lit for each of the eight days of the festival. The special Ḥanukkah candleholder is called a *ḥanukkiah*.

Personal Theme
Religious freedom and dedication. Many Jews become proactive on Hanukkah and engage in projects aimed at obtaining freedom and opportunity for all people.

Traditional Foods
Foods fried in oil, especially potato pancakes (latkes; *levivot* in Hebrew). In Israel, jelly donuts (*sufganiot*) customarily are served.

Customs
1. Each night of Ḥanukkah the *ḥanukkiah* is lit and the appropriate blessings recited (see p. 91 for the Ḥanukkah blessings). The hymn *Ma'oz Tzur* is often chanted after lighting the *ḥanukkiah* (see p. 92).

2. In the synaogogue the *ḥanukkiah* is lit during the *Shaḥarit* (morning) service, but the blessings are not recited.

3. The Torah is read during the morning service. The reading, chapter 7 of the Book of Numbers, tells of the identical gifts brought by the princes of the tribes of Israel at the dedication of the altar.

4. The Hallel psalms of praise are chanted in the synagogue during the morning service. In addition, the special passage *al hanissim* is added to the Amidah prayer. *Al hanissim* thanks God for the miraculous deliverance of our ancestors in other days as well as in our time.

5. Ḥanukkah games are played throughout the festival. The most popular one uses the dreidel, a four-sided spinning top. Each side is marked with a Hebrew letter, either *nun, gimel, hay,* or *shin,* which together stand for the words *Nes gadol hayah sham* ("A

great miracle occurred there"). A player spins the dreidel; if it falls on the *nun,* he or she gets nothing; if it falls on the *gimel,* he or she takes the whole pot; if it falls on the *hay,* the player takes half; if it falls on the *shin,* the player must add to the pot.

6. Sharing and exchanging gifts, including Ḥannukah *gelt* (money).

7. Some people affix a new mezuzah to a doorpost in the home that has yet to receive one (see p. 77 for the blessing). This is an appropriate activity because the word *ḥanukkah* means "dedication," and affixing a mezuzah is the spiritual way to dedicate a room.

8. Some people see Ḥanukkah as the appropriate occasion to affix a *mizraḥ* to an eastern wall in their home. Years ago when the Temple still existed, Jews outside Jerusalem would face the city when praying. For many of the world's Jews, this meant facing eastward. The custom then developed of marking the eastern wall of the home in some manner so that one would always be aware of the direction of Jerusalem. The marker was called a *mizraḥ,* which literally means "east." Today the *mizraḥ* is usually a decoration of some sort; it is hung on the eastern wall of a house or synagogue to indicate the direction of Jerusalem for correct orientation in prayer.

PURIM (Festival of Lots)

Date
Fourteenth of Adar.

Duration
One day.

Source
For that reason these days were named Purim, after *pur.*
—*Esther* 9:26

General Theme
Purim commemorates a miraculous escape from persecution about twenty-four hundred years ago in Persia. Mordecai, a Jewish leader, refused to bow down to Haman, the vizier of King Ahasuerus. Infuriated, Haman obtained permission to exterminate the entire Persian Jewish community and drew lots (*purim* in Hebrew) to determine the day on which the massacre would take place. Through the intervention of Mordecai's niece Queen Esther, the Jews were saved.

Personal Theme
Giving to the poor and sharing food with one's friends.

Traditional Food
Hamantashen (a triangular pastry filled with prunes, poppy seeds, cherries, or the like). The shape of this pastry is reminiscent of the three-cornered hat said to have been worn by Haman.

Customs
1. Some people follow the custom of fasting on the day before Purim. This fast, called the Fast of Esther (*Ta'anit Esther*) is in honor of Esther, who abstained from food for three days before petitioning King Ahasuerus on behalf of her people.

2. The Scroll of Esther (*Megillat Esther*) is publicly chanted aloud both in the evening and the morning. At these services, people are encouraged to masquerade in costume and to use noisemakers (called greggars; *ra'ashanim* in Hebrew) to drown out the name of Haman each time his name is read.

3. Many synagogues and Jewish community centers hold Purim carnivals featuring festive foods, costumes, and carnival games.

4. A festive Purim meal (the Purim *seudah*) is customarily served in the late afternoon. This meal enables family members, relatives, and friends to gather together for a joyous celebration. Merrymaking and general jesting are encouraged in order to heighten the joy at this meal.

5. Sending food baskets (*shalaḥ manot*) to family and friends is an important part of the Purim festival. Making charitable donations is also very much in its spirit.

6. A special passage called *al hanissim* is added during the Amidah prayer, in gratitude to God for the miraculous deliverance of our ancestors in days of old as well as in modern times.

PESAḤ (Passover)

Date
Begins the fourteenth of Nisan.

Duration
Eight days for Conservative, Reconstructionist, and Orthodox Jews. Seven days for Reform Jews and Jews living in Israel.

Names of holiday
1. Feast of Unleavened Bread (*Ḥag HaMatzot*).
2. Holiday of Freedom (*Zeman Ḥeruteinu*).
3. Festival of Spring (*Ḥag He'Aviv*).
Note: The name Passover (Pesaḥ) derives from the Hebrew word *pasach* ("passed over"). The Torah says that the angel of the Lord "passed over" the homes of the Israelites while smiting the firstborn Egyptians (Exodus 12:27).

Source
In the first month, on the fourteenth day of the month, at twilight, there shall be a Passover offering to God, and on the fifteenth day of that month God's Feast of Unleavened Bread. You shall eat unleavened bread for seven days.
—*Leviticus* 23:5

General Theme
This holiday commemorates the Exodus of the Israelites from Egypt under the leadership of Moses some thirty-three hundred years ago.

During their hasty departure, the Israelites did not have time to allow their bread dough to rise. The result was the creation of matzah (unleavened bread), which Jews today eat on Passover as a reminder of our Egyptian slavery. Passover also has an agricultural theme. It heralds the arrival of spring and the beginning of the spring harvest.

Personal Theme
Religious freedom.

Traditional Foods
1. During the Passover Seder meal the following special foods are placed on the Seder plate:

    Haroset: A mixture of chopped nuts, apples, wine, and cinnamon, recalling the mortar used by the Israelite slaves to make bricks for the Egyptian pyramids.

    Roasted bone (*zeroa*): Represents the paschal lamb which was sacrificed by our ancestors.

    Roasted egg (*beitzah*): Symbolizes both the sacrifice made by everyone in the Jerusalem Temple on each holiday and the mourning over the destruction of the Temple.

    Bitter herbs (*maror*): Pure horseradish, to remind us of the bitterness of slavery.

    Parsley (*karpas*): The parsley symbolizes spring and hope for the future. Dipped into salt water, it symbolizes the tears of misery that were shed by our enslaved ancestors.

2. Food that is leavened (*hametz*) may not be eaten on Passover. This includes foods made from wheat, rye, barley, oats, and spelt. Thus biscuits, cakes, cereals, crackers, bread, and liquids made from grain alcohol are expressly forbidden. Foods not *hametz* in and of themselves include meat, fish, fowl, all fruits, all vegetables except peas and beans, and, from freshly opened packages, spices, coffee, tea, sugar, and salt.

All kinds of packaged and prepared foods are available for Passover. To be acceptable, they should carry both the seal of a rabbinic group and the inscription "kosher for Passover" (*kasher l'Pesaḥ*).

Customs

1. Before the festival begins, the house is scrubbed and special care is taken to remove bread and all other *hametz* foods. Special Passover dishes, pots, and dishes are used during the holiday.

2. On the eve of Passover, it is customary to search for any leftover *hametz* in a ceremony called "searching for *hametz*" (*bedikat hametz*). Traditionally the ceremony is conducted with a wooden spoon as a dustpan, a candle for light, and a feather for a broom. The following morning the *hametz* that was gathered during this ceremony is burned.

    All *hametz* that is not burned is stored away in one's home. In many communities this *hametz* is "sold" to a rabbi, who in turn sells *hametz* collectively to a non-Jew. After Passover, the *hametz* reverts to its original owner.

3. A Passover Seder is conducted on the first two nights of Passover (one night for Reform Jews). The text used during the meal at the Seder is the Haggadah.

4. Candles are lit and the appropriate blessing recited on the first two and last two nights of Passover (see p. 46).

5. Historically, "wheat money" (*ma'ot ḥittin*) was given to the poor. Today, it is customary to make a charitable *tzedakah* donation.

6. Beginning on the second night of Passover, Jews begin to count the *omer*. The *omer* (literally "sheaf") refers to an offering from the new barley crop which was brought to the ancient Temple on the eve of the second day of Passover. *Omer* has come to be the name of the period between Passover and Shavuot. By counting the days of this period (*sefirat ha-omer*), we recall the events which

these days connect in the Jewish calendar: the liberation from slavery, commemorated by Passover, and the revelation of the Torah, commemorated by Shavuot. We count the days to heighten our eagerness to celebrate the revelation of the Torah.

7. The first two and last two days of Passover are holy days, with work restrictions. In the synagogue the Hallel psalms of praise are chanted. A special prayer for dew (*Tefillat Tal*) is recited by the cantor at services on the first day of Passover. There are Torah readings on all four of these days. On the first day the reading is Exodus 12:21-51, on the second, Leviticus 22:26-23. The readings for the last two days are Exodus 13:17-15:26 and Deuteronomy 15:19-16:17, respectively.

8. On the evening of the eighth day of Passover it is customary to light a yahrzeit memorial candle in memory of the dead. The following morning during *Shaḥarit* there is a Yizkor memorial service in memory of the departed.

9. Some synagogues follow the custom of reading selections from the *Song of Songs* on the intermediate Sabbath of Passover. Rabbinic tradition interprets the book as a love song, in which the beloved is taken to mean God and the bride to mean the Israelites. This tradition made the book especially appropriate to Passover, because metaphorically the liberation of the Israelites on Passover marked, as it were, the beginning of the courtship of Israel and God, leading to their "marriage" at Mount Sinai when Israel accepted the Torah.

SHAVUOT (Pentecost)

Date
Begins the sixth of Sivan.

Duration
Two days for Conservative, Reconstructionist, and Orthodox Jews. One day for Reform Jews and Jews living in Israel.

Names of holiday
1.   Season of the Giving of Our Torah (*Z'man Matan Torateinu*).
2.   Holiday of First Fruits (*Ḥag Ha-Bikkurim*).

Source
You must count until the day after the seventh week—fifty days; then
you shall bring an offering of new grain to God.
—*Leviticus* 23:16

General Theme
This festival, which occurs seven weeks after the second day of
Passover, commemorates the Israelites' receiving of the Torah at
Mount Sinai. Shavuot, like Passover and Sukkot, is one of the three
Pilgrimage Festivals. In Temple days Israelites brought an offering of
their first fruits (*bikkurim*) to the Temple in Jerusalem. Thus, Shavuot
has also come to be known as the spring harvest festival of first fruits.

Personal Theme
Acceptance of religious obligations (*mitzvot*) and reaffirmation of our
covenant with God.

Traditional Foods
Blintzes, cheesecake, and other dairy foods. The passage "honey and
milk shall be under your tongue" (Song of Songs 4:11) was understood
by our sages to imply that the words of the Torah shall be pleasant
and acceptable to our ears and heart as milk and honey are to our
tongue.

Customs
1.   Candles are lit on both evenings of Shavuot to usher in the holiday
     (for the blessing, see p. 45). This is followed by the festival
     Kiddush over the wine for Shavuot (see p. 92) and the Hamotzi
     blessing over bread (see p. 46).

2.   It is customary to spend many hours on Shavuot night studying
     and discussing Jewish texts. This special gathering for study is
     called *tikkun leil shavuot*; sessions of this kind are held in the
     synagogue and often in private homes as well.

3. Synagogues are usually decorated with greenery and flowers reflecting the harvest aspect of Shavuot.

4. During the morning services, the special Hallel psalms of praise are recited. In addition, the Torah is read on both days of Shavuot. On the first day, the reading includes the Ten Commandments (Exodus 19:1-20:23). On the second day, the reading is from Deuteronomy 15:19-16:17, which includes a description of the three Pilgrimage festivals—Sukkot, Passover, and Shavuot.

5. On the evening of the second night of Shavuot it is customary to light a yahrzeit memorial candle in memory of one's deceased loved ones. At *Shaharit* on the second day there is a Yizkor memorial service.

6. Many synagogues hold a Confirmation service on Shavuot for their Hebrew high school students. The students lead the service and confirm their love for God, Torah, and Israel. They are often presented with Confirmation diplomas.

7. On the first day of Shavuot a special liturgical poem called *Akdamut* is recited at morning services before the Torah reading. The poet, conscious of human inadequacy in praising God, sings the praises of the Creator and of the people Israel's relationship with God.

8. On Shavuot day it is customary to read the Book of Ruth, the story of how Ruth, a Moabite woman, came to embrace the religion of Israel. It includes an account of the grain harvest, and of the treatment of the poor in the harvest season. The book's appropriateness for this holiday is heightened by the tradition that King David, who was descended from Ruth, was born and died on Shavuot.

Other Jewish Commemorations

ROSH ḤODESH (New Month; New Moon)

Date
The first day of every month in the Jewish calendar.

Duration
One or two days. When observed for two days, the first day always falls on the thirtieth of the preceding Hebrew month and the second day falls on the first day of the new month.

Source
On your new moons you shall present a burnt offering to God. — *Numbers* 28:11

General Theme
In biblical times, Rosh Ḥodesh was observed as a holiday accompanied by special sacrificial offerings.

Personal Theme
An opportunity for reflection upon the past month and ways we can improve ourselves in the months to come.

Customs
1. A blessing for the new month is recited on the Sabbath immediately preceding that month (except for the month of Tishri).

2. Hallel psalms of praise are recited during the morning service, and the Torah reading (Numbers 28:1-15) describes the special sacrificial offerings for each new month in biblical times.

TISHA B'AV (Ninth of Av)

Date
Ninth of Av.

Duration
One day.

Theme
Tisha B'Av commemorates the destruction of the First and Second Temples in Jerusalem. The three weeks prior to Tisha B'Av constitute a corresponding period of lesser mourning. During the nine days from the first of Av until and including Tisha B'Av, we remember with sadness the destruction of the Temple. Many people refrain from eating meat during this period (except on the Sabbath), since eating meat was associated with joy.

Customs
1. The fast of Tisha B'Av begins at the end of the evening meal. On the night of Tisha B'Av the lights are dimmed in the synagogue. Congregants often sit on low benches (or on the floor). In this mourning posture they follow the reading from the Book of Lamentations (*Eikhah*) by candlelight or with a flashlight.

2. During morning services the next day, the prayers are spoken rather than chanted. Tefillin and tallit are not worn. The Torah reading is taken from Deuteronomy 4:25-40. The Haftarah, taken from the Book of Jeremiah (8:13-9:23), opens with the words, "I will utterly consume them, says God."

3. In the afternoon, during the Minḥah service, the mood begins to change. Both tallit and tefillin are worn. The Torah (Exodus 32:11-14, 34:1-10) and Haftarah (Isaiah 55:6-56:8) are read.

4. Eating and drinking, bathing and conjugal relations are forbidden during the commemoration of Tisha B'Av.

TU BESHEVAT (Jewish Arbor Day)

Date
Fifteenth of Shevat.

Duration
One day.

Name of holiday
New Year for Trees (*Rosh HaShanah L'ilanot*).

Source
Mentioned in the Mishnah (*Rosh Hashanah* 1:1).

Theme
Tu Beshevat commemorates the beginning of the spring season in Israel, when the trees begin to blossom. The official organization responsible for planting trees in Israel is called the Jewish National Fund (*Keren Kayemet L'Yisrael*). In Israel children and adults plant trees on this holiday. In the Diaspora it is customary to purchase Jewish National Fund certificates.

Traditional Foods
Fruits and vegetables are customarily eaten on Tu Beshevat. These include Israeli fruits mentioned in the Bible, including grapes, pomegranates, figs, dates, olives, and *bokser* (St. John's Bread), the fruit of the carob tree.

Customs
1. Many synagogues and families hold a Tu Beshevat Seder using four cups of wine (one white, symbolizing winter; the second, light red symbolizing spring; the third, deep red symbolizing summer; and the fourth, red mixed with white symbolizing fall). A Tu Beshevat Haggadah is commonly used to recite blessings over the various fruits and reminds us of the importance of trees.

2. In Israel, children plant saplings in the Jewish National Fund forests. In Western countries it is customary to purchase tree certificates in honor and memory of friends and relatives.

YOM HASHOAH *(Holocaust Memorial Day)*

Date
Twenty-seventh of Nisan.

Duration
One day.

Theme
A day to recall the six million Jews of Europe who were tortured and murdered during the Second World War because they were Jews. We recall the beauty of their lives as well as the horror of their deaths.

Customs
1. A synagogue community memorial service is held, commemorating the martyred dead. Holocaust survivors and their children often speak at the service. A six-branched candelabrum is lit in commemoration of the six million.

2. A selection of readings relating to Holocaust themes is read during the memorial service. The *Eil Malei* prayer in memory of the six million and the Mourner's Kaddish are generally recited as well.

YOM HAZIKARON *(Remembrance Day)*

Date
Fourth of Iyar.

Duration
One day.

Theme
An Israeli memorial day observed for soldiers killed in defense of Israel from the War of Independence (1948) through the present day. It is observed with solemn civil, military, and religious ceremonies throughout Israel.

Customs

1. Memorial candles are lit in army camps, schools, synagogues, and public places, and flags are flown at half-mast.

2. Throughout the day ex-servicemen and soldiers serve as guards of honor at war memorials in all towns and villages. Families of the fallen participate in memorial ceremonies at military cemeteries.

3. All places of entertainment are closed on the eve of Yom HaZikaron.

4. In the morning sirens mark a two-minute silence throughout the country which brings all activity to a standstill.

5. Special services on Yom HaZikaron (and also on the preceding Sabbath) include Psalm 9 ("For the leader, on the death of the son") and Psalm 144 ("Blessed be God, my Rock, who trains my hands for war and my fingers for battle").

YOM HA-ATZMA'UT (Israel Independence Day)

Date
Fifth of Iyar.

Duration
One day.

Theme
Commemorates the establishment of the State of Israel on May 14, 1948, corresponding to the fifth of Iyar, 5708.

Traditional Foods
Israel foods, such as pita, falafel, and humus.

Customs
1. Public gatherings and celebrations take place, including an Israel Day parade in New York City and in other communities, usually held on the Sunday closest to the fifth of Iyar.

2. Included in the synagogue prayers of the day are the Hallel psalms of praise and the addition of *al hanissim* in the Amidah, thanking God for Israel's miraculous deliverance.

LAG B'OMER (Thirty-third Day of the Omer)

Date
Eighteenth of Iyar.

Duration
One day.

Theme
The days between Passover and Shavuot are a solemn period recalling the suffering which the Jews endured under Roman persecution. Lag B'Omer breaks the series of solemn days. According to Jewish folklore, this is because Bar Kokhba won a great victory over the Romans on the thirty-third day of the *omer*. Another tradition relates that on this day a plague that was raging among Rabbi Akiba's students suddenly stopped.

Name
Scholars' Holiday

Customs
1. Weddings are often held on Lag B'Omer, because of the joyousness of the day.

2. Picnics, outings, games with bows and arrows, sporting events, and bonfires are popular ways of celebrating.

3. Traditional Jews often give their children their first haircut on Lag B'Omer. This custom came about because the days before Lag B'Omer were days of mourning and haircutting was not permitted, so Lag B'Omer afforded the first new opportunity to cut hair.

Summary of Jewish Holidays and Their Dates

Approximate English date	Hebrew date	Holiday
September	29 Elul (evening)	⚱ Eve of Rosh Hashanah (New Year)
	1 Tishri	⚱ First day, Rosh Hashanah
	2 Tishri	Second Day, Rosh Hashanah
September-	9 Tishri (evening)	⚱ Kol Nidre, opening prayer of Yom
October	10 Tishri	Kippur (Day of Atonement)
October	14 Tishri	⚱ Eve of Sukkot
	15 Tishri	⚱ First Day, Sukkot (Tabernacles)
	16 Tishri	Second Day, Sukkot
	21 Tishri	⚱ Eve of Hoshanah Rabbah
	22 Tishri	⚱ Shemini Atzeret (Feast of Conclusion, Eighth Day of Solemn Assembly)
	23 Tishri	Simḥat Torah (rejoicing of the Law)
December	24 Kislev (evening) to 1 Tevet	First Hanukkah light (eight nights in all)
January	15 Shevat	Tu BeShevat (New Year of the trees)
March	13 Adar	Eve of Purim (Megillah reading)
	14 Adar	Purim

March-April	14 Nisan	🕯 Passover, first Seder (evening)
	15 Nisan	🕯 Second Seder
	20 Nisan	🕯 Eve of
	21 Nisan	🕯 Concluding days of Passover seventh day
	22 Nisan	Eighth day
April-May	16 Nisan to	Counting the Omer (49 days,
	5 Sivan	no weddings)
	27 Nisan	Remembrance Day (Yom Hashoah, memorializing victims of the Holocaust)
	5 Iyyar	Israel Independence Day (Yom Ha'atzma'ut)
	18 Iyyar	Lag b'Omer (33rd day of Counting the Omer, weddings allowed)
May-June	5 Sivan (evening)	🕯 Eve of Shavuot, Bikkurim
	6 Sivan	🕯 First day, Shavuot (Feast of Weeks or First Fruits)
	7 Sivan	Second Day, Shavuot
August	9 Av	Tishah b'Av (Feast of the Ninth of Av, commemorating the destruction of the Temple)

🕯 Candles lit

Starting A Jewish Home

By wisdom is a house built, and by understanding it is established.
—Proverbs 24:3

Judaism is a home-centered way of life. Every holiday and festival, with its home rituals, special foods, music, songs, and stories, can bring joy and delight to your family, and beauty and holiness to living as a Jew.

The Jewish home has traditionally been referred to as a miniature sanctuary (*mikdash me'at*) marked by serenity and holiness. Whether or not you and your family build a sanctuary together depends on the choices you make.

On the following pages you will find some of Judaism's basic home rituals and observances. They will help you on your way.

Remember that you need not start by doing all of them at once. Start with whatever custom or ritual appeals to you. Once you are comfortable with it, try adding some additional ones.

Affixing The Mezuzah

Write them on the doorposts of your house, and
on your gates.
—Deuteronomy 6:9

Because of the centrality of the Jewish home, Judaism has developed a housewarming ceremony known as *ḥanukkat habayit* to be enacted whenever a family begins life in a new home. Bread and salt, symbols of fertility and prosperity, are often used during this formal dedication of a family's new home. In addition mezuzot are affixed to the doorposts of the house. A mezuzah is a container made of metal, ceramic, or wood. Inside it is a special parchment scroll on which two passages from the Torah are written, Deuteronomy 6:4-9 and Deuteronomy 11:13-21. The container itself usually has the word *Shaddai*("Almighty") or the Hebrew letter *shin* displayed on the front.

The mezuzah is placed on the doorpost on the right-hand side as one enters. It is fastened diagonally, on the upper third of the doorpost, the top slanted toward the house or room. Before affixing the mezuzah, say this blessing:

בָּרוּךְ אַתָּה יהוה אֱלֹהֵינוּ מֶלֶךְ הָעוֹלָם, אֲשֶׁר קִדְּשָׁנוּ בְּמִצְוֹתָיו, וְצִוָּנוּ לִקְבּוֹעַ מְזוּזָה.

Barukh atah adonai eloheinu melekh ha-olam asher kid'shanu b'mitzvotav v'tzivanu likbo'a mezuzah.

Praised are You, Eternal our God, Sovereign of the Universe whose mitzvot add holiness to our lives, and who gave us the mitzvah of affixing a mezuzah.

How To Make Shabbat At Home

Call the Sabbath a delight.

—Isaiah 53:13

Preparing For Shabbat

The Sabbath is portrayed in the Jewish mystical tradition as a bride or queen who visits Jewish homes every week throughout the year. It is important to properly prepare both physically and spiritually to greet the honored guest.

As the week draws to a close, preparations for the Sabbath intensify. The house is cleaned, Shabbat candlesticks and wine cup are polished, the table is set with the best dinnerware, and festive food and sacramental wine are made ready. To add to the mood of caring and sharing, families often drop some coins in a *tzedakah* (charity) box before candlelighting.

Lighting The Shabbat Candles

The Sabbath begins about twenty minutes before sundown on Friday. Its start is heralded by the lighting of at least two candles, symbolizing the two biblical formulations of the Sabbath commandment: "Remember the Sabbath day" (Exodus 20:8) and "Observe the Sabbath day" (Deuteronomy 5:12). In some households one candle is lit for each member of the family.

Some people follow the custom of moving their hands around the flames several times and bringing them to their face. This gesture symbolically welcomes the Sabbath into the home. Before reciting the blessing, it is customary to cover the eyes.

בָּרוּךְ אַתָּה יהוה אֱלֹהֵינוּ מֶלֶךְ הָעוֹלָם, אֲשֶׁר קִדְּשָׁנוּ בְּמִצְוֹתָיו,
וְצִוָּנוּ לְהַדְלִיק נֵר שֶׁל שַׁבָּת.

*Barukh atah adonai eloheinu melekh ha-olam asher kid'shanu
b'mitzvotav v'tzivanu lehadlik ner shel shabbat.*

Praised are You, Eternal our God, Sovereign of the Universe
whose mitzvot add holiness to our lives, and who gave us the
mitzvah to kindle Shabbat light.

Family Blessings

It is customary for parents to bless their children before sitting
down to the Sabbath meal. This provides them with an opportunity
to express appreciation for their children, something they may not
always have time for during a busy week. Through the touch of your
hands and the sound of your voice, your children can feel and respond
to the love and affection you have for them.

For Boys: Gently place both of your hands on the child's head and
recite:

יְשִׂימְךָ אֱלֹהִים כְּאֶפְרַיִם וְכִמְנַשֶּׁה.

Yesimkha elohim k'ephrayim v'khi-menasheh.

May God give you the blessings of Ephraim and Manasseh.

For Girls: Gently place both of your hands on the head and recite:

יְשִׂימֵךְ אֱלֹהִים כְּשָׂרָה, רִבְקָה, רָחֵל, וְלֵאָה.

Yesimekh elohim k'sarah, rivkah, rachel, v'leah.

May God give you the blessings of Sarah, Rebekah, Rachel, and
Leah.

*For both boys and girls, conclude with the priestly blessing (Numbers
6:24-26):*

יְבָרֶכְךָ יהוה וְיִשְׁמְרֶךָ.
יָאֵר יהוה פָּנָיו אֵלֶיךָ וִיחֻנֶּךָ.
יִשָּׂא יהוה פָּנָיו אֵלֶיךָ וְיָשֵׂם לְךָ שָׁלוֹם.

Yevarekhekha adonai ve-yishmerekha.
Ya'er adonai panav elekha vi-ḥuneka.
Yisa adonai panav elekha ve-yasem lekha shalom.

May God bless you and guard you.
May God show you favor and be gracious to you.
May God show you kindness and grant you peace.

Eishet Chayil, taken from the Book of Proverbs (31:10-31), is a hymn of praise customarily sung by the husband to honor the wife.

אֵשֶׁת־חַיִל מִי יִמְצָא
וְרָחֹק מִפְּנִינִים מִכְרָהּ:
בָּטַח בָּהּ לֵב בַּעְלָהּ
וְשָׁלָל לֹא יֶחְסָר:
גְּמָלַתְהוּ טוֹב וְלֹא רָע
כֹּל יְמֵי חַיֶּיהָ:
דָּרְשָׁה צֶמֶר וּפִשְׁתִּים
וַתַּעַשׂ בְּחֵפֶץ כַּפֶּיהָ:
הָיְתָה כָּאֳנִיּוֹת סוֹחֵר
מִמֶּרְחָק תָּבִיא לַחְמָהּ:
וַתָּקָם בְּעוֹד לַיְלָה
וַתִּתֵּן טֶרֶף לְבֵיתָהּ
וְחֹק לְנַעֲרֹתֶיהָ:

Eishet ḥayil mi yimtza
v'raḥok mip'ninim mikharah.
Bataḥ bah lev ba'lah
v'shalal lo yeḥsar.
G'malat'hu tov v'lo ra
kol y'mei ḥayeha.
Darsha tzemer u-fishtim
vata'as b'ḥefetz kape'ha.

Hay'ta ko'oniyot soḥer
mimerḥak tavi laḥmah.
Vatakom b'od lailah
vatiten teref l'veita
v'ḥok l'na'aroteha.

A good wife, who can find?
She is more precious than rubies.
The heart of her husband trusts in her
And he has no lack of gain.
She does him good and not harm
All the days of her life.
She seeks wool and flax,
And works willingly with her hands.
She is like the merchant ships
She brings her food from afar.
She rises also while it is yet night,
And gives food to her household,
And a portion to her maidens.

For those who would like an analagous selection on praise of the husband, we include the following suggested reading (Psalms 112).

הַלְלוּיָהּ
אַשְׁרֵי־אִישׁ יָרֵא אֶת־יְיָ
בְּמִצְוֺתָיו חָפֵץ מְאֹד:
גִּבּוֹר בָּאָרֶץ יִהְיֶה זַרְעוֹ
דּוֹר יְשָׁרִים יְבֹרָךְ:
הוֹן־וָעֹשֶׁר בְּבֵיתוֹ
וְצִדְקָתוֹ עֹמֶדֶת לָעַד:
זָרַח בַּחֹשֶׁךְ אוֹר
לַיְשָׁרִים.

Hal'luyah.
Ashrei ish yarei et Adonai
b'mitzvotav ḥafetz m'od.
Gibor ba'aretz yiyeh zaro
dor y'sharim y'vorakh.
Hon va'osher b'veito

v'tzid'kato omedet la'ad,
Zarah ba'hoshekh or
la-y'sharim.

Halleluya! Happy is the man who reveres Adonai,
Who greatly delights in God's commandments.
His descendents will be honored in the land,
The generation of the upright will be praised.
His household prospers and his righteousness lasts forever.
Light shines in the darkness for the upright.

Friday Night Blessing Over Wine (Kiddush)

Because happiness and joy are synonymous with the Sabbath, it is customary to begin the meal by reciting the Kiddush, a blessing over the wine. In this act of sanctification, we thank God for having created the grapes from which wine is made. We also praise God for creating the world, delivering us from Egypt, and giving us the holy Sabbath.

(וַיְהִי עֶרֶב וַיְהִי בֹקֶר)

יוֹם הַשִּׁשִּׁי, וַיְכֻלּוּ הַשָּׁמַיִם וְהָאָרֶץ וְכָל־צְבָאָם. וַיְכַל אֱלֹהִים
בַּיּוֹם הַשְּׁבִיעִי מְלַאכְתּוֹ אֲשֶׁר עָשָׂה, וַיִּשְׁבֹּת בַּיּוֹם הַשְּׁבִיעִי מִכָּל־
מְלַאכְתּוֹ אֲשֶׁר עָשָׂה. וַיְבָרֶךְ אֱלֹהִים אֶת־יוֹם הַשְּׁבִיעִי וַיְקַדֵּשׁ
אֹתוֹ, כִּי בוֹ שָׁבַת מִכָּל־מְלַאכְתּוֹ אֲשֶׁר בָּרָא אֱלֹהִים לַעֲשׂוֹת.

Vay'hi erev vay'hi voker—
Yom ha-shi-shi. Vay'khulu ha-shamayim v'ha-aretz v'khol tz'va-
am. Vay'khal elohim ba-yom ha-sh'vi-i m'lakh-to asher asah,
va-yishbot ba-yom ha-sh'vi-i mikol m'lakh-to asher asah. Vay'va-
rekh elohim et yom ha-sh'vi-i vay'kadesh oto, ki vo shavat mikol
m'lakh-to asher bara elohim la-ot.

And there was morning and there was evening—
the sixth day. The heavens and the earth, and all they contain, were completed. On the seventh day God completed the work which He had been doing; He ceased on the seventh day from all the work which He had done. Then God blessed the seventh day and called it holy, because on it He ceased from all His work of Creation.

בָּרוּךְ אַתָּה יהוה אֱלֹהֵינוּ מֶלֶךְ הָעוֹלָם, בּוֹרֵא פְּרִי הַגָּפֶן.
בָּרוּךְ אַתָּה יהוה אֱלֹהֵינוּ מֶלֶךְ הָעוֹלָם, אֲשֶׁר קִדְּשָׁנוּ בְּמִצְוֹתָיו
וְרָצָה בֶנוּ, וְשַׁבָּת קָדְשׁוֹ בְּאַהֲבָה וּבְרָצוֹן הִנְחִילָנוּ, זִכָּרוֹן לְמַעֲשֵׂה
בְרֵאשִׁית. כִּי הוּא יוֹם תְּחִלָּה לְמִקְרָאֵי קֹדֶשׁ, זֵכֶר לִיצִיאַת מִצְרָיִם,
כִּי בָנוּ בָחַרְתָּ וְאוֹתָנוּ קִדַּשְׁתָּ מִכָּל־הָעַמִּים, וְשַׁבָּת קָדְשְׁךָ בְּאַהֲבָה
וּבְרָצוֹן הִנְחַלְתָּנוּ. בָּרוּךְ אַתָּה יהוה, מְקַדֵּשׁ הַשַּׁבָּת.

*Barukh atah adonai eloheinu melekh ha-olam, borey pri hagafen.
Barukh atah adonai eloheinu melekh ha-olam asher kid'shanu
b'mitzvotav veratzah vanu, v'shabbat kodsho be'ahavah uv'ratson
hinhilanu, zikkaron l'ma-aseh v'reisheet. Ki hu yom tehilah l'mik-
ra-ei kodesh zekher litziat mitzrayim. Ki vanu vaharta v'otanu
kidashta mikol ha'amim, v'shabbat kod-shekha b'ahavah
uv'ratzon hinhal-tanu. Barukh atah adonai m'kaddesh ha-
shabbat.*

Praised are You, Eternal our God, Sovereign of the Universe who
creates the fruit of the vine.

Praised are You, Eternal our God, Sovereign of the Universe
whose mitzvot add holiness to our lives, cherishing us through the
gift of the holy Shabbat granted lovingly, gladly, a reminder of
Creation. It is the first among our days of sacred assembly which
recall the Exodus from Egypt. Thus You have chosen us,
endowing us with holiness, from among all peoples by granting
us Your holy Shabbat lovingly and gladly. Praised are You,
Eternal, who hallows Shabbat.

Shalom Aleikhem — Peace be unto you

We welcome the Sabbath by singing this hymn which welcomes the
angels of peace.

שָׁלוֹם עֲלֵיכֶם. מַלְאֲכֵי הַשָּׁרֵת. מַלְאֲכֵי עֶלְיוֹן.
מִמֶּלֶךְ מַלְכֵי הַמְּלָכִים. הַקָּדוֹשׁ בָּרוּךְ הוּא:
בּוֹאֲכֶם לְשָׁלוֹם. מַלְאֲכֵי הַשָּׁלוֹם. מַלְאֲכֵי עֶלְיוֹן.
מִמֶּלֶךְ מַלְכֵי הַמְּלָכִים. הַקָּדוֹשׁ בָּרוּךְ הוּא:

בָּרְכוּנִי לְשָׁלוֹם. מַלְאֲכֵי הַשָּׁלוֹם. מַלְאֲכֵי עֶלְיוֹן.
מִמֶּלֶךְ מַלְכֵי הַמְּלָכִים. הַקָּדוֹשׁ בָּרוּךְ הוּא:
צֵאתְכֶם לְשָׁלוֹם. מַלְאֲכֵי הַשָּׁלוֹם. מַלְאֲכֵי עֶלְיוֹן.
מִמֶּלֶךְ מַלְכֵי הַמְּלָכִים. הַקָּדוֹשׁ בָּרוּךְ הוּא:

Shalom aleikhem malakhei hashareit malakhei elyon
Mimelekh malakhei ham'lakhim hakadosh barukh hu

Boakhem l'shalom malakhei hashalom malakhei elyon
Mimelekh malakhei ham'lakhim hakadsoh barukh hu

Barkhuni l'shalom malakhei hashalom malakhei elyon
Mimelekh malakhei hamlakhim hakadosh barukh hu.

Tzeitkhem leshalom malakhei hashalim malakhei elyon
Mimelekh malakhei hamlakhim hakadosh barukh hu.

We wish you peace, attending angels, angels of the most sublime, the Sovereign of sovereigns, the Holy One.

Come to us in peace, angels of peace, angels of the most sublime, the Sovereign of sovereigns, the Holy One.

Bless us with peace, angels of peace, angels of the most sublime, the Sovereign of sovereigns, the Holy One.

Take your leave in peace, angels of peace, angels of the most sublime, the Sovereign of sovereigns, the Holy One.

Washing The Hands

Netilat yadayim, the ritual washing of the hands, follows the recitation of Kiddush. Just as the ancient priests cleansed their hands before performing their duties in the Temple, we wash our hands to sanctify the act of eating.

Washing the hands can be done over the kitchen sink or a large basin. A cup or pitcher of water is held in the left hand and poured over the right. The process is reversed and repeated once or twice.

The following blessing is recited:

בָּרוּךְ אַתָּה יהוה אֱלֹהֵינוּ מֶלֶךְ הָעוֹלָם, אֲשֶׁר קִדְּשָׁנוּ בְּמִצְוֹתָיו,
וְצִוָּנוּ עַל נְטִילַת יָדָיִם.

*Barukh atah adonai eloheinu melekh ha-olam, asher kid'shanu
b'mitzvotav v'tzivanu al netilat yadayim.*

Praised are You, Eternal our God, Sovereign of the Universe
whose mitzvot add holiness to our lives, and who gave us the
mitzvah of washing the hands.

Blessing Over Bread

The bread eaten on Shabbat and Jewish holidays is usually a braided
loaf called a *hallah*. It is traditional to place two hallot on the table to
recall the double portion of manna God provided for the Israelites in
the desert on the sixth day of the week because no manna fell on the
Sabbath. A cloth is spread over the *hallot* to symbolize the dew that
covered the manna. The covering is removed after Kiddush and the
washing of hands, and the following blessing, known as *Hamotzi*, is
said:

בָּרוּךְ אַתָּה יהוה אֱלֹהֵינוּ מֶלֶךְ הָעוֹלָם, הַמּוֹצִיא לֶחֶם מִן הָאָרֶץ.

*Barukh atah adonai eloheinu melekh ha-olam, hamotzi lehem
min ha-aretz.*

Praised are You, Eternal our God, Sovereign of the Universe who
brings forth bread from the earth.

Blessings After The Meal

The Bible says, "When you have eaten your fill, give thanks to God
for the good land which God has given you" (Deuteronomy 8:10).
This passage provides the basis for the blessing after the meal. There
are several versions of the blessing. The shorter form is included here.

רַבּוֹתַי נְבָרֵךְ.

Rabotai nevaraykh
Friends, let us give thanks.

The others respond, and the leader repeats:

יְהִי שֵׁם יהוה מְבֹרָךְ מֵעַתָּה וְעַד עוֹלָם.

Yehi shem adonai mevorakh may'atah v'ad olam.

May the Eternal be praised now and forever.

The leader continues:

בִּרְשׁוּת רַבּוֹתַי, נְבָרֵךְ (אֱלֹהֵינוּ) שֶׁאָכַלְנוּ מִשֶּׁלּוֹ.

Bireshut rabotai nevaraykh (eloheinu) she-akhalnu mishelo.

With your consent friends, let us praise (our God) the One of whose food we have partaken.

The others respond, and the leader repeats:

בָּרוּךְ (אֱלֹהֵינוּ) שֶׁאָכַלְנוּ מִשֶּׁלּוֹ וּבְטוּבוֹ חָיִינוּ.

Barukh (eloheinu) she-akhalnu mishelo uv'tuvo ḥayinu.

Praised be (our God) the One of whose food we have partaken and by whose goodness we live.

Leader and others:

בָּרוּךְ הוּא וּבָרוּךְ שְׁמוֹ.

Barukh hu uvarukh sh'mo.

Praised be God and praised be God's name.

בָּרוּךְ אַתָּה יהוה אֱלֹהֵינוּ מֶלֶךְ הָעוֹלָם, הַזָּן אֶת־הָעוֹלָם כֻּלּוֹ
בְּטוּבוֹ, בְּחֵן בְּחֶסֶד וּבְרַחֲמִים. הוּא נוֹתֵן לֶחֶם לְכָל־בָּשָׂר כִּי לְעוֹלָם
חַסְדּוֹ. וּבְטוּבוֹ הַגָּדוֹל תָּמִיד לֹא חָסַר לָנוּ וְאַל יֶחְסַר לָנוּ מָזוֹן

לְעוֹלָם וָעֶד בַּעֲבוּר שְׁמוֹ הַגָּדוֹל, כִּי הוּא אֵל זָן וּמְפַרְנֵס לַכֹּל
וּמֵטִיב לַכֹּל וּמֵכִין מָזוֹן לְכָל־בְּרִיּוֹתָיו אֲשֶׁר בָּרָא. בָּרוּךְ אַתָּה
יהוה, הַזָּן אֶת־הַכֹּל.

*Barukh atah adonai eloheinu melekh ha-olam, hazan et ha-olam
kulo b'tuvo b'hen, b-hesed, u-v'rahamim. Hu notayn lehem
l'khol basar, ki l'olam hasdo. Uv'tuvo hagadol, tamid lo hasar
lanu, v'al yehsar lanu mazon l'olam va-ed, ba-avur sh'mo
hagadol, ki hu el zan um'farnays lakol, umaytiv lakol, umaykhin
mazon le-khol beriyotav asher bara. Barukh atah adonai, hazan
et hakol.*

Praised are You, Eternal our God, Sovereign of the Universe who
sustains the whole world with kindness and compassion. You
provide food for every creature, for Your love endures forever.
Your great goodness has never failed us. Your great glory assures
us nourishment. All life is God's creation and God is good to all,
providing every creature with food and sustenance. Praised are
You, Eternal who sustains all life.

נוֹדֶה לְךָ יהוה אֱלֹהֵינוּ עַל שֶׁהִנְחַלְתָּ לַאֲבוֹתֵינוּ אֶרֶץ חֶמְדָּה טוֹבָה
וּרְחָבָה, בְּרִית וְתוֹרָה, חַיִּים וּמָזוֹן. יִתְבָּרַךְ שִׁמְךָ בְּפִי כָל־חַי תָּמִיד
לְעוֹלָם וָעֶד, כַּכָּתוּב: וְאָכַלְתָּ וְשָׂבָעְתָּ וּבֵרַכְתָּ אֶת־יהוה אֱלֹהֶיךָ
עַל הָאָרֶץ הַטּוֹבָה אֲשֶׁר נָתַן לָךְ. בָּרוּךְ אַתָּה יהוה, עַל הָאָרֶץ
וְעַל הַמָּזוֹן.

*Nodeh l'kha adonai eloheinu al she-hinhalta la-avoteinu eretz
hemdah, tovah ur'havah, brit v'torah, hayim umazon. Yit-
barakh shim-kha b'fi khol hai tamid l'olam va'ed. Ka-katuv
v'akhalta v'savata u-vayrakhta et adonai elo-hekha al ha-aretz
hatovah asher natan lakh. Barukh atah adonai, al ha-aretz v'al
hamazon.*

We thank You, Eternal our God, for the pleasing, ample, desirable
land which You gave to our ancestors, for the covenant and
Torah, for life and sustenance. May You forever be praised by all
who live, as it is written in the Torah: "When you have eaten and
are satisfied, you shall praise the Eternal your God for the good
land which He has given you." Praised are You, Eternal, for the
land and for sustenance.

וּבְנֵה יְרוּשָׁלַיִם עִיר הַקֹּדֶשׁ בִּמְהֵרָה בְיָמֵינוּ. בָּרוּךְ אַתָּה יהוה,
בּוֹנֵה בְרַחֲמָיו יְרוּשָׁלַיִם, אָמֵן.

Uv'neih yerushala-yim ir hakodesh bim'heirah v'yameinu. Barukh atah adonai, boneh v'rahamav yerushala-yim. Amen.

Fully rebuild Jerusalem, the holy city, soon in our time. Praised are You, Eternal who in mercy rebuilds Jerusalem. Amen.

בָּרוּךְ אַתָּה יהוה, אֱלֹהֵינוּ מֶלֶךְ הָעוֹלָם, הַמֶּלֶךְ הַטּוֹב וְהַמֵּטִיב
לַכֹּל. הוּא הֵטִיב, הוּא מֵטִיב, הוּא יֵיטִיב לָנוּ. הוּא גְמָלָנוּ, הוּא
גוֹמְלֵנוּ, הוּא יִגְמְלֵנוּ לָעַד לְחֵן וּלְחֶסֶד וּלְרַחֲמִים וִיזַכֵּנוּ לִימוֹת
הַמָּשִׁיחַ.

Barukh atah adonai, elohaynu melekh ha-olam, hamelekh hatov v'hameitiv lakol. Hu heitiv, hu meitiv, hu yeitiv lanu. Hu g'malanu, hu gomleinu, hu yigm'leinu la-ad l'hen u-l'hesed u-l'rahamim, viyzakeinu li-ymot hamashiah.

Praised are You, Eternal our God, Sovereign of the Universe who is good to all, whose goodness is constant through all time. Favor us with kindness and compassion now and in the future as in the past. May we be worthy of the days of the Messiah.

הָרַחֲמָן, הוּא יַנְחִילֵנוּ יוֹם שֶׁכֻּלּוֹ שַׁבָּת וּמְנוּחָה לְחַיֵּי הָעוֹלָמִים.

Harahaman hu yan-hileinu yom shekulo shabbat umenuhah l'ha-yei ha-olamim.

May the Merciful grant us a day of true Shabbat rest, reflecting the life of eternity.

וְנִשָּׂא בְרָכָה מֵאֵת יהוה וּצְדָקָה מֵאֱלֹהֵי יִשְׁעֵנוּ וְנִמְצָא חֵן וְשֵׂכֶל
טוֹב בְּעֵינֵי אֱלֹהִים וְאָדָם. עֹשֶׂה שָׁלוֹם בִּמְרוֹמָיו, הוּא יַעֲשֶׂה
שָׁלוֹם עָלֵינוּ וְעַל כָּל־יִשְׂרָאֵל, וְאִמְרוּ אָמֵן.

V'nisa v'rakhah mei-eit adonai u-tzedakah mei-elohei yisheinu v'nimtza ḥen v'seikhel tov b'einei elohim v'adam. Oseh shalom bim'romav hu ya-aseh shalom aleinu v'al kol yisrael. V'imru amen.

May we receive blessings from the Eternal, loving-kindness from the God of our deliverance, finding grace and good favor with God and mortals. May God who brings peace to the universe bring peace to us and to all the people Israel. And let us say: Amen.

Havdalah

The ritual conclusion of the Sabbath is deferred until about an hour after sunset, to make the sweetness of the day last as long as possible. When three stars are visible in the evening sky it is time for the Havdalah service.

הִנֵּה אֵל יְשׁוּעָתִי, אֶבְטַח וְלֹא אֶפְחָד. כִּי עָזִּי וְזִמְרָת יָה יהוה, וַיְהִי לִי לִישׁוּעָה. וּשְׁאַבְתֶּם מַיִם בְּשָׂשׂוֹן מִמַּעַיְנֵי הַיְשׁוּעָה. לַיהוה הַיְשׁוּעָה, עַל עַמְּךָ בִרְכָתֶךָ סֶּלָה. יהוה צְבָאוֹת עִמָּנוּ, מִשְׂגָּב לָנוּ אֱלֹהֵי יַעֲקֹב, סֶלָה. יהוה צְבָאוֹת, אַשְׁרֵי אָדָם בּוֹטֵחַ בָּךְ. יהוה הוֹשִׁיעָה, הַמֶּלֶךְ יַעֲנֵנוּ בְיוֹם קָרְאֵנוּ.

Hinei eil yeshuatee, evtaḥ v'lo efḥad. Ki azi v'zimrat yah adonai, vay'hi li lishua. Ush'avtem mayim b'sason mi-may'nei ha-y'shuah. Ladonai ha-y'shuah, al amḥa virkha-tekha selah. Adonai tzeva'ot imanu, misgav lanu elohei ya'akov selah. Adonai tzevaot, ashrei adam botei-aḥ bakh. Adonai hoshiyah, hamelekh ya'aneinu v'yom koreinu.

Behold, God is my deliverance. I am confident and unafraid. Adonai is my strength, my might, my deliverance. With joy shall you draw water from the wells of deliverance. Deliverance is the Eternal's; You will bless Your people. Adonai tzeva'ot is with us; the God of Jacob is our fortress. Adonai tzeva'ot, blessed the one who trusts in You. Help us, Eternal; answer us, Sovereign, when we call.

All together:

לַיְּהוּדִים הָיְתָה אוֹרָה וְשִׂמְחָה וְשָׂשׂוֹן וִיקָר. כֵּן תִּהְיֶה לָנוּ.

Lay'hudim haytah orah v'simḥah v'sasson vikar. Kein tih-yeh lanu.

Grant us the blessings of light, of gladness, and of honor which the miracle of deliverance brought to our ancestors.

The person leading the Havdalah ceremony raises the cup of wine and says:

כּוֹס יְשׁוּעוֹת אֶשָּׂא וּבְשֵׁם יהוה אֶקְרָא.

Kos y'shuot esa, uv'shem adonai ekra.

I will lift the cup of deliverance and call upon the Eternal.

Blessing over wine:

בָּרוּךְ אַתָּה יהוה אֱלֹהֵינוּ מֶלֶךְ הָעוֹלָם, בּוֹרֵא פְּרִי הַגָּפֶן.

Barukh atah adonai eloheinu melekh ha-olam, borei pri hagafen.

Praised are You, Eternal our God, Sovereign of the Universe who creates the fruit of the vine.

Next, lift the spice box and say:

בָּרוּךְ אַתָּה יהוה אֱלֹהֵינוּ מֶלֶךְ הָעוֹלָם, בּוֹרֵא מִינֵי בְשָׂמִים.

Barukh atah adonai eloheinu melekh ha-olam, borei minei v'samim.

Praised are You, Eternal our God, Sovereign of the Universe who creates fragrant spices.

The leader sniffs the spices and passes the spice box around for everyone to share.

Next, the leader recites the blessing over the light, while all hold out their hands with palms up and look at the reflection of the flame on their fingernails. In this way everyone makes use of the light.

בָּרוּךְ אַתָּה יהוה אֱלֹהֵינוּ מֶלֶךְ הָעוֹלָם, בּוֹרֵא מְאוֹרֵי הָאֵשׁ.

Barukh atah adonai eloheinu melekh ha-olam, borei m'orei ha-esh.

Praised are You, Eternal our God, Sovereign of the Universe who creates the lights of fire.

בָּרוּךְ אַתָּה יהוה אֱלֹהֵינוּ מֶלֶךְ הָעוֹלָם, הַמַּבְדִּיל בֵּין קֹדֶשׁ לְחוֹל, בֵּין אוֹר לְחְשֶׁךְ, בֵּין יִשְׂרָאֵל לָעַמִּים, בֵּין יוֹם הַשְּׁבִיעִי לְשֵׁשֶׁת יְמֵי הַמַּעֲשֶׂה. בָּרוּךְ אַתָּה יהוה, הַמַּבְדִּיל בֵּין קֹדֶשׁ לְחוֹל.

Barukh atah adonai eloheinu melekh ha-olam, ha-mavdil bein kodesh l'khol, bein or l'hoshekh, bein yisrael la-amim, bein yom ha-sh'vi-i l'shei-shet y'mei ha-ma-aseh. Barukh atah adonai, hamavdil bein kodesh l'khol.

Praised are You, Eternal our God, Sovereign of the Universe who has endowed all creation with distinctive qualities, distinguishing between sacred and secular time, between light and darkness, between the people Israel and the other peoples, between the seventh day and the six working days of the week. Praised are You, Eternal who distinguishes between secular and sacred time.

Exchange greetings of Shavua Tov ("Have a good week").

Other Home Rituals

Lighting The Ḥanukkiah

Rock of Ages, let our song praise Your saving power.
—Ḥanukkah hymn

We light one candle on the first night of Ḥanukkah and add an additional candle each subsequent night. The candles are added from right to left as seen when facing the *ḥanukkiah* (the Ḥanukkah candleholder).

On the first night, put one candle on the right-hand side of the *ḥanukkiah* (on the second night, put one candle on the right-hand side, another directly to its left, and so on for the subsequent nights). Then light the *shamash* (the candle used to light the others), take it in your hand, and say:

בָּרוּךְ אַתָּה יהוה אֱלֹהֵינוּ מֶלֶךְ הָעוֹלָם, אֲשֶׁר קִדְּשָׁנוּ בְּמִצְוֹתָיו וְצִוָּנוּ לְהַדְלִיק נֵר שֶׁל חֲנֻכָּה.

Barukh atah adonai eloheinu melekh ha-olam, asher kid'shanu b'mitzvotav v'tzivanu l'hadlik ner shel ḥanukkah.

Praised are You, Eternal our God, Sovereign of the Universe whose mitzvot add holiness to our life, and who gave us the mitzvah to light the lights of Ḥanukkah.

בָּרוּךְ אַתָּה יהוה אֱלֹהֵינוּ מֶלֶךְ הָעוֹלָם, שֶׁעָשָׂה נִסִּים לַאֲבוֹתֵינוּ בַּיָּמִים הָהֵם וּבַזְּמַן הַזֶּה.

Barukh attah adonai eloheinu melekh ha-olam, sheh-asah nissim la-avoteinu ba-yamim ha-heim u-va-z'man ha-zeh.

Praised are You, Eternal our God, Sovereign of the Universe who
accomplished miracles for our ancestors in ancient days, and in
our time.

On the first night of Ḥanukkah, the following is added:

בָּרוּךְ אַתָּה יהוה אֱלֹהֵינוּ מֶלֶךְ הָעוֹלָם, שֶׁהֶחֱיָנוּ וְקִיְּמָנוּ וְהִגִּיעָנוּ
לַזְּמַן הַזֶּה.

Barukh atah adonai eloheinu melekh ha-olam, sheh-heh-heh-ya-
nu v'keey'manu v'hee-gee-anu lazman hazeh.

Praised are You, Eternal our God, Sovereign of the Universe, for
granting us life, for sustaining us, and for enabling us to reach this
day.

Ma'oz Tzur has been a popular Ḥanukkah hymn for many
centuries and is sung in most households.

מָעוֹז צוּר יְשׁוּעָתִי לְךָ נָאֶה לְשַׁבֵּחַ.
תִּכּוֹן בֵּית תְּפִלָּתִי וְשָׁם תּוֹדָה נְזַבֵּחַ.
לְעֵת תָּכִין מַטְבֵּחַ מִצָּר הַמְנַבֵּחַ.
אָז אֶגְמוֹר בְּשִׁיר מִזְמוֹר חֲנֻכַּת הַמִּזְבֵּחַ.

Ma-oz tzur y'shuatee, l'kha na'eh l'shabeiaḥ
Tikon beit t'fillatee, v'sham todah n'zabeiaḥ
L'eit takhin matbeiaḥ mitzar ham'nabeiaḥ
Az egmor b'shir mizmor ḥanukkat hamizbeiaḥ.

Rock of Ages, let our song praise Your saving power.
You amid the raging throng were our sheltering tower.
Furious they assailed us, but Your help availed us.
And Your word broke their sword when our own strength
failed us.

Kiddush For Festivals

If festival is Friday evening, add the following:

(וַיְהִי עֶרֶב וַיְהִי בֹקֶר)

יוֹם הַשִּׁשִּׁי, וַיְכֻלּוּ הַשָּׁמַיִם וְהָאָרֶץ וְכָל־צְבָאָם. וַיְכַל אֱלֹהִים
בַּיּוֹם הַשְּׁבִיעִי מְלַאכְתּוֹ אֲשֶׁר עָשָׂה, וַיִּשְׁבֹּת בַּיּוֹם הַשְּׁבִיעִי מִכָּל־
מְלַאכְתּוֹ אֲשֶׁר עָשָׂה. וַיְבָרֶךְ אֱלֹהִים אֶת־יוֹם הַשְּׁבִיעִי, וַיְקַדֵּשׁ
אֹתוֹ, כִּי בוֹ שָׁבַת מִכָּל־מְלַאכְתּוֹ אֲשֶׁר בָּרָא אֱלֹהִים לַעֲשׂוֹת.

Vay'hi erev vay'hi voker—
Yom ha-shi-shi. Vay'khulu ha-shamayim v'ha-aretz v'khol tz'va-
am. Vay'khal elohim ba-yom ha-sh'vi-i m'lakh-to asher asah, va-
yishbot ba-yom ha-sh'vi-i mikol m'lakh-to asher asah. Vay'va-
rekh elohim et yom ha-sh'vi-i vay'kadesh oto, ki vo shavat mikol
m'lakh-to asher bara elohim la-asot.

And there was morning and there was evening—
the sixth day. The heavens and the earth, and all they contain,
were completed. On the seventh day God completed the work
which He had been doing; He ceased on the seventh day from
all the work which He had done. Then God blessed the seventh
day and called it holy, because on it He ceased from all His work
of Creation.

בָּרוּךְ אַתָּה יהוה אֱלֹהֵינוּ מֶלֶךְ הָעוֹלָם, בּוֹרֵא פְּרִי הַגָּפֶן.

בָּרוּךְ אַתָּה יהוה אֱלֹהֵינוּ מֶלֶךְ הָעוֹלָם, אֲשֶׁר בָּחַר בָּנוּ מִכָּל־עָם
וְרוֹמְמָנוּ מִכָּל־לָשׁוֹן, וְקִדְּשָׁנוּ בְּמִצְוֹתָיו. וַתִּתֶּן לָנוּ יהוה אֱלֹהֵינוּ
בְּאַהֲבָה (שַׁבָּתוֹת לִמְנוּחָה וּ) מוֹעֲדִים לְשִׂמְחָה, חַגִּים וּזְמַנִּים
לְשָׂשׂוֹן, אֶת־יוֹם (הַשַּׁבָּת הַזֶּה וְאֶת־יוֹם)
חַג הַמַּצּוֹת הַזֶּה, זְמַן חֵרוּתֵנוּ,
חַג הַשָּׁבוּעוֹת הַזֶּה, זְמַן מַתַּן תּוֹרָתֵנוּ,
חַג הַסֻּכּוֹת הַזֶּה, זְמַן שִׂמְחָתֵנוּ,
הַשְּׁמִינִי, חַג הָעֲצֶרֶת הַזֶּה, זְמַן שִׂמְחָתֵנוּ,
(בְּאַהֲבָה) מִקְרָא קֹדֶשׁ, זֵכֶר לִיצִיאַת מִצְרָיִם. כִּי בָנוּ בָחַרְתָּ וְאוֹתָנוּ

קִדַּשְׁתָּ מִכָּל־הָעַמִּים, (וְשַׁבָּת) וּמוֹעֲדֵי קָדְשְׁךָ (בְּאַהֲבָה וּבְרָצוֹן)
בְּשִׂמְחָה וּבְשָׂשׂוֹן הִנְחַלְתָּנוּ. בָּרוּךְ אַתָּה יהוה, מְקַדֵּשׁ (הַשַּׁבָּת וְ)
יִשְׂרָאֵל וְהַזְּמַנִּים.

Barukh atah adonai eloheinu melekh ha-olam, borei pri hagafen.
Barukh atah adonai eloheinu melekh ha-olam, asher bahar
banu mikol am v'ro-m'manu mikol lashon vekid'shanu
b'mitzvotav, vatiten lanu adonai elohenu b'ahavah (shabbatot
lim'nuhah u) mo-adim l'simhah hagim uzmanim l'sasson, et
yom (ha-shabbat hazeh v'et yom)

> Passover: *hag ha-matzot hazeh, z'man hei-ruteinu*
> Shavuot: *hag ha-shavuot hazeh, z'man matan torateinu*
> Sukkot: *hag ha-sukkot hazeh, z'man simhateinu*
> Shemini Atzeret and Simhat Torah: *ha-sh'mini hag ha'atzeret*
> *hazeh, z'man simhateinu*

(b'ahavah) mikra kodesh zekher litziat mitzrayim. Ki vanu
vaharta v'otanu kidashta mikol ha'amim (v'shabbat) u-mo-adei
kodshekha (b'ahavah uv'ratzon) b'simhah uv'sasson hin-haltanu.
Barukh atah adonai, m'kadesh (ha-shabbat v') yisrael
v'hazmanim.

Praised are You, Eternal our God, Sovereign of the Universe who
creates fruit of the vine.

Praised are You, Eternal our God, Sovereign of the Universe who
has chosen and distinguished us from among all others by adding
holiness to our lives with mitzvot. Lovingly have You given us
(Shabbat for rest,) festivals for joy and holidays for happiness,
among them this (Shabbat and this) day of
> *On Passover:* Pesah, season of our liberation,
> *On Shavuot:* Shavuot, season of the giving of the Torah,
> *On Sukkot:* Sukkot, season of our joy,
> *On Shemini Atzeret and Simhat Torah:* Shemini Atzeret,
> season of our joy,
a day of sacred assembly recalling the Exodus from Egypt. Thus
You have chosen us, endowing us with holiness from among all

peoples by granting us (Shabbat and) Your hallowed festivals (lovingly and gladly) in happiness and joy. Praised are You, God who hallows (Shabbat and) the people Israel and the festivals.

Candlelighting Blessing for Festivals

בָּרוּךְ אַתָּה יהוה אֱלֹהֵינוּ מֶלֶךְ הָעוֹלָם, אֲשֶׁר קִדְּשָׁנוּ בְּמִצְוֹתָיו וְצִוָּנוּ לְהַדְלִיק נֵר שֶׁל (שַׁבָּת וְשֶׁל) יוֹם טוֹב.

Barukh atah adonai eloheinu melekh ha-olam, asher kid'shanu b'mitzvotav v'tzivanu l'hadlik ner shel (shabbat v'shel) yom tov.

Praised are You, Eternal our God, Sovereign of the Universe whose mitzvot add holiness to our lives, and who gave us the mitzvah to kindle light for (Shabbat and for) the festival.

Prayer Chart Summary

Here is a brief summary of twelve basic daily prayers. The background of each prayer is presented along with some of the concepts it stresses. Page numbers refer to pagination in *Siddur Sim Shalom*.

Mah Tovu (p. 2)

מַה טֹּבוּ אֹהָלֶיךָ יַעֲקֹב מִשְׁכְּנֹתֶיךָ יִשְׂרָאֵל.

Mah tovu ohalekha ya'akov mish-k'notekha yisrael.

How lovely are your abodes, people of Jacob, your dwelling places, descendants of Israel. (Numbers 24:5)

Background
The first verse (Numbers 24:5) was originally recited by Balaam, a non-Jewish prophet hired by Balak, the king of Moab. Balaam intended to curse the Israelites, but when he saw their camp from a nearby hilltop, he felt compelled to bless them instead: "How lovely (*ma tovu*) are your tents, people of Jacob, your dwelling places, descendants of Israel."

Concepts
We focus on the need to worship God with reverence and love. Then we are ready to proceed with the service of prayer.

Birkhot Hashaḥar (p. 10)

Background
Originally these fifteen blessings were written for use at home during the regular morning routine of arising, washing, dressing, and so forth.

Later, because many people did not know them, the morning
blessings were recited by a leader in the synagogue, where everyone
could feel included by responding Amen.

Concepts
The routines in our lives, no matter how mundane, are never to be
taken for granted.

Barukh She'amar (p. 54)

בָּרוּךְ שֶׁאָמַר וְהָיָה הָעוֹלָם.

Barukh she'amar v'haya ha-olam.

Praised be God who created the world with His word.

Background
This prayer in praise of God, first mentioned in the ninth century,
introduces the morning service.

Concepts
1. We praise God for having created the world by God's word.
2. We praise God for the wonder of the world, and for the creative
    power making possible all that we see and experience.

Ashrei (p. 80)

אַשְׁרֵי יוֹשְׁבֵי בֵיתֶךָ עוֹד יְהַלְלוּךָ סֶּלָה.

Ashrei yoshvei veite-kha od y'hal'lukha, selah.

Happy are they who live in Your house,
They shall continue to praise You. (Psalm 84:5)

Background
Ashrei consists of Psalm 145 and a brief introduction from two other

psalms. The Talmud (*Berakhot* 4b) states that "whoever says this psalm three times daily will be assured of a place in the world-to-come." The focus of *Ashrei* is the verse "You open Your hand and satisfy all living things with favor." Psalm 145 is an alphabetical acrostic, each verse beginning with a different letter of the Hebrew alphabet in sequence, with the exception of *nun*, which is omitted.

Concepts
1. Dwelling in God's house is a blessing.
2. God's concern extends to the oppressed and the poor.

Psalm 150 (p. 88)

Background
In ancient times, instrumental music was part of the worship service in the Temple. The instruments used included the ones mentioned in this psalm. When the Temple was destroyed, the use of musical instruments in Jewish worship ended, as a way of mourning its destruction. The Hebrew word *halleluyah*, which means "praise God," appears in various forms a total of thirteen times in this psalm.

Concepts
We can praise God in ways other than verbal prayer, including dance, song, and playing musical instruments.

Barkhu (p. 96)

בָּרְכוּ אֶת יְהֹוָה הַמְּבֹרָךְ.

Bar'khu et Adonai ha-m'vorakh

Praised be the Eternal, Source of blessing.

Background
In ancient times the high priest would call the people to prayer in the Jerusalem Temple with the words of *Barkhu.*

Concepts
God is praised as the Source of all blessings.

Or Ḥadash/Ahavah Rabbah (p. 98)

Background
Or Ḥadash (meaning "a new light") is known as the *Yotzer* or Creation blessing. In it we praise God for having created lights. *Ahavah Rabbah* (meaning "deep love") celebrates the giving of the Torah, an act that shows God's love for the people of Israel.

Both of these blessings act as a prelude to the *Sh'ma* which follows. They are intended to negate the idea that there are different powers controlling various aspects of creation. God is the sole Creator.

Concepts
1. God is the Creator and Source of all light.
2. God shows us love by giving us the Torah and asking us to perform mitzvot.
3. We praise God for having chosen us to be a special people by giving us mitzvot (commandments) to fulfill.

Sh'ma Yisrael (pp. 100-102)

שְׁמַע יִשְׂרָאֵל יְהֹוָה אֱלֹהֵינוּ יְהֹוָה אֶחָד:

Sh'ma Yisrael Adonai elohenu Adonai eḥad.

Hear, O Israel: Adonai is Our God, Adonai is One. (Deuteronomy 6:4)

Background
In ancient times *Sh'ma Yisrael* was recited publicly in the Temple after the recitation of the Ten Commandments. Later it became the core of the synagogue service. Some people cover their eyes when they say the words of the *Sh'ma*, as a way of increasing their level of concentration.

Concepts

1. The first passage of the *Sh'ma* (Deuteronomy 6:4-9) affirms that God alone is to be our God, and that we should love God with all of our power and might. As a reminder of our love for God, we place the words of the *Sh'ma* on our doorposts (on the parchment in the mezuzah) and on our arms and foreheads (by wearing tefillin).

2. In the second passage of the *Sh'ma* (Deuteronomy 11:13-21) the Israelites are told that if they obey God's commandments, there will be ample rain. But if they worship other gods, the rain will stop and they will perish. In order to serve as a reminder of the promise and the warning, "these words" are to be inserted in the capsules of the tefillin and inscribed on the parchment of the mezuzah.

3. In the third passage of the *Sh'ma* (Numbers 15:37-41) a reference is made to the fringes (*tzitzit*) which the Israelites are to put on their garments. This ritual apparel refers to the prayer shawl or tallit, whose fringes are visual reminders to perform God's commandments.

Mi Khamokha (p. 104)

Background

When the people of Israel left Egypt and crossed the Red Sea, they sang the song "Who is like You, God, among all that is worshiped?" (Exodus 15:11).

Concepts

1. This song praises God for doing wonders, and affirms that God is unique and unlike any other.
2. The song concludes with the blessing after the *Shema* which praises God as the Redeemer of Israel.

Amidah (pp. 106-120)

Background
The Amidah ("Standing [Prayer]") is central to the Jewish liturgy. Also known as HaTefillah ("*The* Prayer") and as the Shemoneh Esrei ("Eighteen Benedictions"), it is included in varying forms in every worship service.

Concepts
Today there are nineteen rather than eighteen benedictions in the weekday Amidah, but the name *Shemoneh Esrei* is still widely used.
1. *Avot* ("Ancestors"): God is the God of our ancestors, was their protector and is ours.
2. *Gevurot* ("Power"): God's power in nature is great, and extends to giving life to the dead.
3. *Kedushah* ("Sanctification"): God is unique, holy.
4. *Da'at* ("Knowledge"): We petition God for knowledge and understanding.
5. *Teshuvah* ("Repentance"): We ask God to accept our repentance.
6. *Selihah* ("Forgiveness"): We ask God to grant us forgiveness.
7. *Geulah* ("Redemption"): We praise God for redeeming the Israelites.
8. *Refuah* ("Healing"): We praise God for healing our people and ask that we be healed.
9. *Birkat HaShanim* ("Blessing the Years"): We praise God for satisfying us with abundance and blessing the years.
10. *Kibbutz Galuyot* ("Ingathering of the Exiles"): We praise God for gathering the dispersed.
11. *Tzedakah Umishpat* ("Justice and Mercy"): We ask God to sustain us with justice and mercy.
12. *Malshinim* ("Maligners"): We ask God to humble the arrogant and frustrate the hopes of those who malign us.
13. *Tzaddikim* ("Righteous People"): We ask God to sustain the righteous.
14. *Yerushalayim* ("Jerusalem"): We ask God to build Jerusalem.
15. *David* ("David"): We ask God to bring to flower the shoot of David and assure our deliverance.

16. *Shome'a Tefillah* ("Listen to Our Prayers"): We ask God to hear our prayer.
17. *Avodah* ("Worship"): We ask God to accept our worship.
18. *Hoda'ah* ("Thanksgiving"): We thank God for the daily miracles of life, and acknowledge their source.
19. *Shalom* ("Peace"): We praise God and pray for peace.

Aleinu (p. 160)

עָלֵינוּ לְשַׁבֵּחַ לַאֲדוֹן הַכֹּל לָתֵת גְּדֻלָּה לְיוֹצֵר בְּרֵאשִׁית

Aleinu l'sha-bei-aḥ la'adon hakol latayt gedulah l'yotzer beresheet.

It is our duty to praise the Master of all, to acclaim the Creator.

Background
Aleinu is an ancient prayer that originally was a part of the Musaf service for Rosh HaShanah. For the last six centuries it has been included at the end of all prayer services in the synagogue. One tradition ascribes the authorship to Rav, a third-century rabbi.

Concepts
1. In the first passage, we praise God as Creator of the universe and for choosing the Israelites for their special destiny. It is customary to bend the knee and bow at the Hebrew words *va'anaḥnu korim u'mishtaḥavim* ("we bend the knee and bow").

2. The second passage stresses a universal theme. It concludes with a verse from the prophet Zechariah (14:9), who envisions a time when all people will acknowledge God as the One God.

Adon Olam (p. 6)

אֲדוֹן עוֹלָם אֲשֶׁר מָלַךְ, בְּטֶרֶם כָּל יְצִיר נִבְרָא.

Adon olam, asher malakh b'terem kol y'tzir nivra.

The Master of the universe ruled before anything was created.

Background
One tradition ascribes the authorship of *Adon Olam* to the eleventh-century Spanish poet Solomon ibn Gabirol. Although *Adon Olam* is included at the beginning of the morning service, it is generally used as a concluding hymn.

Concepts
1. God is eternal.
2. God is Sovereign of the world and our Protector.
3. One need not fear by day or by night, since we are in God's constant care.

Time Line of Jewish Personalities and Events

Date B.C.E.	Event	Important People
1900	Abraham begins to worship one God.	Abraham and Sarah Isaac and Rebekah
1750	During famine, Abraham's great-grandchildren leave Israel and go to Egypt.	Jacob, Rachel, and Leah; Joseph
1450	Ten plagues; Pharaoh releases Israelite slaves; Israelites wander in desert forty years.	Moses, Miriam, Aaron
1410-1050	Israelites conquer Canaan, settle down in tribes ruled by judges	Joshua, Deborah, Samson
1050-933	Saul unifies tribes; David enlarges kingdom; Solomon builds First Temple.	Samuel, Saul, David, Solomon, Nathan
928	Kingdom splits in two: Israel in north, Judea in south. Prophets attempt to teach people to listen to Elijah, Amos, Micah	
722	Assyria conquers northern kingdom, takes its people away as captives.	Isaiah

586	Babylonians conquer Judea and destroy Temple; Babylonian Exile begins.	Jeremiah, Ezekiel
538	Cyrus permits return to Judea; Temple rebuilt.	Esther, Ezra, Nehemiah
322	Judea becomes immersed in Greek culture (Hellenism)	
168-164	Antiochus driven out by Maccabees; Temple cleansed.	Hannah, Mattathias, Judah Maccabee
63	Romans conquer Judea.	Herod

C.E.

30	Romans kill Jesus. His followers begin to spread Christianity throughout empire.	Hillel and Shammai, Philo
66-73	Jewish revolt against Rome; last Jewish rebels die at Masada.	Simeon bar Giora, Johanan ben Zakkai,
132-135	Second Jewish revolt against Rome. Jews continue to pray and study secretly.	Akiva ben Joseph, Bar Kokhba, Meir, Beruriah, Simeon bar Yohai
210	Center of Jewish study shifts to Babylonia. Mishnah edited by Judah Ha-Nasi.	Judah Ha-Nasi, Samuel
400-500	Babylonian Jews build academies, Gemara completed.	Rav Ashi, Rabina
622	Muhammad founds Islam in Arabia.	

740-970	Judaism spreads as far as Russia, where Khazar kingdom converts	Saadia Gaon, Ḥasdai ibn Shaprut
950-1391	Spain is new center of Jewish life; Jews become doctors, scientists, poets.	Samuel ha-Nagid, Solomon ibn Gabirol, Judah Halevi, Moses ibn Ezra
950-1100	Jews settle in England, France, and Germany, where Gershom and Rashi study and comment on Jewish law. Maimonides major Jewish philosopher in Egypt.	Gershom ben Judah, Rashi, Maimonides
1096-1320	Crusaders drive Muslims out of Palestine, destroy many Jewish communities there and on way.	Meir of Rothenberg
1200-1400	Jews persecuted in Western Europe.	
1348-1349	Black Plague. Increasing oppression in Spain.	Moses de Leon, Solomon ibn Adret, Joseph Albo
1492	Expulsion of Jews from Spain; those who remain practice Judaism secretly as Marranos.	
1500-1600	Spanish and Portuguese Jews flee to Italy, North Africa, Balkans, New World. Find welcome in Turkish Empire and Palestine. Code of Jewish law completed by Joseph Caro.	Gracia Mendes, Joseph Nasi, Joseph Caro

1400-1648	Jews live peacefully in Poland, governed by Council of the Four Lands.	Moses Isserles, Solomon Luria
1648-1658	Cossacks in Poland revolt, destroy hundreds of Jewish communities.	
1665-1676	False Messiah Shabbetai Zevi brings hope to desperate Polish Jews; is imprisoned and forced to become Muslim.	Shabbetai Zevi
1500-1700	Marranos move north to Holland and France to practice Judaism freely; Jews begin return to England.	Manasseh ben Israel
1654	Twenty-three Jews come to New Amsterdam from Brazil.	Asser Levy, Jacob Barsimson
1750s ·	Hasidism emerges as religious revolt.	Israel Ba'al Shem Tov, Shneur Zalman of Liady, Vilna Gaon, Moses Mendelssohn
1787	U.S. Constitution promises religious freedom to all. France gives equal rights to Jews	Haym Salomon, Aaron Lopez, Rebecca Gratz
1800-1900	Equal rights spread in Western Europe; pogroms in Eastern Europe.	Moses Montefiore, Mayer Rothschild, Judah Leib Gordon, Sholem Aleichem

1881	Pogroms in Russia, Jews begin emigrating to Western Europe and America. First modern Zionists go to Palestine.	Edmond de Rothschild, Moses Hess
1894	Dreyfus falsely accused of treason in France.	
1897	First Zionist Congress.	Leo Pinsker, Theodor Herzl
1900-1914	Pogroms drive more Russian Jews to Western Europe, America, and Palestine.	Emma Lazarus, Lillian Wald
1917	Britain issues Balfour Declaration, more Jews settle in Palestine.	Aḥad Ha-Am Louis D. Brandeis
1933	Nazis gain power in Germany; Jews persecuted.	Leo Baeck, Stephen S. Wise, Henrietta Szold
1939-1945	World War II. By 1945, six million Jews are killed.	Mordecai Anielewicz, Janusz Korczak
1948	State of Israel established.	David Ben-Gurion, Chaim Weizmann
1967	Israel wins Six-Day War, Jerusalem reunified	Moshe Dayan, Yigal Allon
1973	Yom Kippur War	Golda Meir, Arik Sharon
1979	Egypt and Israel sign Camp David Accords.	Menahem Begin
1980s	Mass exodus of Ethiopian and Soviet Jews.	

Suggested Readings

Reading and studying Jewish books will help you maintain a high level of Jewish literacy and make you feel more secure in your Jewishness. Here are some suggested readings for further study.

General

Encyclopaedia Judaica. Jerusalem: Keter, 1972.
  Excellent full-scale English-language encyclopedia of Judaism that is all-encompassing.

Glustrom, Simon. *Language of Judaism.* Northfield, NJ: Jason Aronson, 1988.
  An easy-to-read book that reveals the meaning of a variety of terms and concepts vital to an understanding of Judaism.

Kling, Simcha. *Embracing Judaism.* New York: Rabbinical Assembly, 1987.
  An excellent introductory text to teach values, rituals, and history of Jewish tradition.

Kolatch, Alfred J. *The Jewish Book of Why.* 2 vols. New York: Jonathan David, 1981, 1985.
  Provides answers to hundreds of questions related to Judaism.

————. *The Jewish Home Advisor.* New York: Jonathan David, 1990.
  A guide to the performance of all Jewish customs and ceremonies.

————. *The Name Dictionary.* New York: Jonathan David, 1967.
  A comprehensive dictionary of Hebrew names and their English equivalents.

Olitzky, Kerry M., and Ronald H. Isaacs. *A Glossary of Jewish Life.* Northfield, NJ: Jason Aronson, 1992.
A comprehensive Jewish dictionary of words, concepts, and values.

Trepp, Leo. *The Complete Book of Jewish Observance.* New York: Behrman House and Summit Books, 1980.
A one-volume guide to the ceremonies and practices of Judaism.

Conservative Judaism

Dorff, Elliot. *Conservative Judaism: Our Ancestors to Our Descendants.* New York: United Synagogue, 1977.
A sourcebook on the development and structure of Conservative Judaism, including chapters on Jewish law and basic Jewish beliefs.

Emet Ve-emunah: Statement of Principles of Conservative Judaism. New York: Jewish Theological Seminary, Rabbinical Assembly, and United Synagogue of America, 1988.
Conservative Jewish views on God, the Jewish people, and living a life of Torah.

Gordis, Robert. *Understanding Conservative Judaism.* New York: Rabbinical Assembly, 1978.
A guide to Conservative Judaism and exploration of the meaning and content of the movement.

Siegel, Seymour, ed. *Conservative Judaism and Jewish Law.* New York: Rabbinical Assembly, 1977.
Essays and responsa on the unique approach of Conservative Judaism to Jewish law and its development.

Waxman, Mordecai, ed. *Tradition and Change.* New York: Rabbinical Assembly, 1958.
Explains Conservative Judaism as seen in the classic statements of its founders and leading spokespersons.

Jewish Practice

Dresner, Samuel. *The Sabbath.* New York: Burning Bush Press, 1970.
Insightful analysis of the concept of the Sabbath and its influence
throughout the centuries.

Goodman, Philip, ed. *The Hanukkah Anthology.* Philadelphia: Jewish
Publication Society, 1976.
The seven holiday anthologies by Goodman are useful guides for
the meaningful celebration of the Jewish festivals.

————, ed. *The Passover Anthology.* Philadelphia: Jewish Publication
Society, 1961.

————, ed. *The Purim Anthology.* Philadelphia: Jewish Publication
Society, 1949.

————, ed. *The Rosh HaShanah Anthology.* Philadelphia: Jewish
Publication Society, 1970.

————, ed. *The Shavuot Anthology.* Philadelphia: Jewish Publication
Society, 1975.

————, ed. *The Sukkot and Simhat Torah Anthology.* Philadelphia:
Jewish Publication Society, 1973.

————, ed. *The Yom Kippur Anthology.* Philadelphia: Jewish Publication Society, 1971.

Harlow, Jules, ed. *The Bond of Life: A Book for Mourners.* New York:
Rabbinical Assembly, 1983.
Prayerbook and guide for the Jewish mourner.

————, ed. *Siddur Sim Shalom.* New York: Rabbinical Assembly and
United Synagogue of America, 1985.
Newest Conservative prayerbook.

Isaacs, Ronald. *Bride and Groom Handbook.* New York: Behrman House, 1987.
    A primer that will help a Jewish couple prepare for marriage.

———. *How to Book for Jewish Living.* Hoboken: Ktav, 1992.
    Fact-filled how-to manual containing all the basic things that a Jew needs to know to live a Jewish life.

———. *Rites of Passage: A Guide to the Jewish Life Cycle.* Hoboken: Ktav, 1992.
    Useful guide for understanding the concepts and rituals of the religious milestones in the life of a Jew.

———. *Shabbat Delight: A Celebration in Stories, Games and Songs.* Hoboken: Ktav, 1987.
    Multimedia kit containing Sabbath stories, songs, games, and a how-to manual for Shabbat observance.

———and Kerry M. Olitzky. *A Jewish Mourner's Handbook.* Hoboken: Ktav, 1991.
    A guide for the bereaved.

Klein, Isaac. *A Guide to Jewish Religious Practice.* Augmented ed. New York: Jewish Theological Seminary, 1992.
    Code of Jewish law for the Conservative Jew.

Lebeau, James M. *Sanctify Life.* New York: United Synagogue of America, 1983.
    Excellent sourcebook on the Jewish dietary laws and their rationale.

Riemer, Jack, ed. *Jewish Reflections on Death.* New York: Schocken, 1976.
    Excellent treatment of the Jewish way of death and mourning and the psychological wisdom of the related laws.

Siegel, Seymour, and Samuel H. Dresner. *The Jewish Dietary Laws.* New York: Rabbinical Assembly and United Synagogue Commission on Jewish Education, 1982.
Guide to the Jewish dietary laws and their observance.

Wolfson, Ron. *The Art of Jewish Living: Hanukkah.* Los Angeles: Federation of Jewish Men's Club and University of Judaism, 1990.
Sensitively deals with the traditions of Hanukkah as well as with the variety of ways in which modern Jews grapple with the complex emotions and celebrations of the Christmas and Hanukkah seasons.

————. *The Art of Jewish Living: The Shabbat Seder.* Los Angeles: Federation of Jewish Men's Clubs and University of Judaism. 1985.
Excellent introduction to the observance of Shabbat and an explanation of its customs and rituals.

Jewish Thought

Gertel, Elliot, and Seymour Siegel, eds. *God in the Teachings of Conservative Judaism.* New York: Rabbinical Assembly, 1985.
Essays by leading Conservative thinkers on theological approaches to understanding God.

Gillman, Neil. *Sacred Fragments.* Philadelphia: Jewish Publication Society, 1990.
Addresses difficult theological questions and presents answers.

Heschel, Abraham J. *Between God and Man.* New York: Free Press, 1959.
Spiritually uplifting writings.

Liturgy

Arzt, Max. *Joy and Remembrance: Commentary on the Sabbath Liturgy.* New York: Hartmore House, 1979.
Commentary on the Sabbath service.

————. *Justice and Mercy: A Commentary on Liturgy of the New Year and the Day of Atonement.* Holt, Rinehart & Winston, 1963.
   Excellent guide to the High Holy Day liturgy.

Brown, Steven. *Higher and Higher: Making Jewish Prayer a Part of Us.* New York: United Synagogue, 1979.
   Sourcebook for understanding the nature of Jewish prayer and the development of the prayerbook.

Garfiel, Evelyn. *Service of the Heart: A Guide to the Jewish Prayerbook.* Northfield, NJ: Jason Aronson, 1989.
   Basic guide to understanding Jewish prayers and the prayerbook.

Glossary

Judaism has its own vocabulary, including terms for customs and ceremonies, holidays, rituals, and life-cycle events. Many terms and phrases are in Hebrew or Yiddish. The more terms that you can identify, the more comfortable and confident you will feel.

This is a beginner's list of frequently used words and phrases. Use it as a reference. With time and experience most of them will become a basic part of your own vocabulary of life.

Synagogue Terms

Aliyah. The honor of being called to recite the Torah blessings during a synagogue Torah reading.

Aron HaKodesh. "Holy ark." The receptacle in which the Torah scrolls are kept.

Beit Knesset. "House of assembly." The synagogue.

Bimah. Platform-pulpit area in a synagogue.

Haftarah. "Conclusion." The prophetic section recited after the reading of the Torah on Sabbaths, festivals, and other occasions.

Ḥazzan. Cantor.

Kippah. Skullcap.

Maḥzor. (1) Prayerbook used on Rosh HaShanah and Yom Kippur. (2) Special prayerbook for one of the three Pilgrimage Festivals.

Minyan. Quorum of ten adults needed for a public prayer service.

Ner Tamid. "Eternal light." Light above the ark which is always kept burning.

Oneg Shabbat. "Shabbat joy." Celebration after Friday evening services which often includes refreshments, singing, Israeli dancing, and discussions.

Sefer Torah. The Torah scroll, consisting of the Five Books of Moses: Genesis, Exodus, Leviticus, Numbers, and Deuteronomy.

Shul. Synagogue (Yiddish).

Siddur. Prayerbook.

Sidrah. The weekly portion of the Torah that is read aloud at services.

Tallit. Prayer shawl worn during morning prayer services and on Kol Nidrei eve.

Holiday Terms

Shabbat

Besamim. Spices used during the Havdalah service.

Ḥallah. See Food terms.

Erev Shabbat. The eve of the Sabbath (Friday evening).

Hamotzi. Blessing said over bread.

Havdalah. "Separation." Service on Saturday night bidding farewell to the Sabbath.

Kabbalat Shabbat. "Welcoming the Sabbath." Service just before the evening service on Friday night.

Kiddush. "Sanctification." Blessing over wine.

Motza-ey Shabbat. The "departure" of the Sabbath.

Seudah Shelisheet. "Third meal" eaten during late Sabbath afternoon.

Shabbat Shalom. "Sabbath Peace." A Sabbath greeting.

Shaharit. The morning service.

Shomer Shabbat. A Sabbath observer.

Zemirot. Sabbath (or festival) songs sung at the table.

Rosh Hashanah and Yom Kippur

Al Heit. Opening words, and hence the title, of Yom Kippur confessional prayer.

Aseret Y'may Teshuvah. The Ten Days of Repentance from Rosh HaShanah to Yom Kippur. Also known as the Days of Awe.

Baal Toke'ah. Person who sounds the shofar.

Gemar hatimah tovah. "May your final verdict be a favorable one." Greeting for the days after Rosh HaShanah.

High Holy Days. Rosh HaShanah and Yom Kippur, and the days in between.

Kol Nidrei. Liturgical text which ushers in Yom Kippur.

Leshanah tovah tikateivu. "May you be inscribed for a good year." Greeting for Rosh HaShanah.

Mahzor. Festival prayerbook.

Neilah. Closing service of Yom Kippur.

Selihot. (1) Prayers of forgiveness recited during High Holy Days. (2) Penitential prayer service beginning at midnight on Saturday preceding Rosh HaShanah. If Rosh HaShanah falls on Tuesday or earlier in week, the recitation of Selichot begins on Sunday morning of preceding week.

Shofar. Ram's horn.

Shevarim. Three blasts of the shofar.

Tekiah. One blast of the shofar.

Tekiah Gedolah. One very long shofar blast.

Teruah. Nine short blasts of the shofar.

Teshuvah. Repentance.

Yamim Noraim. The Days of Awe. The ten days of repentance from Rosh HaShanah to Yom Kippur. Also known as Aseret Y'may Teshuvah.

Sukkot, Shemini Atzeret, Simhat Torah

Aravot. Long narrow willow leaves attached to *lulav.*

Etrog. Citron, one of Four Species used during Sukkot.

Four Species (*Arba Minim*). Collective term for *etrog, lulav, aravot* (willows), and *hadassim* (myrtle) used on Sukkot.

Hadassim. Myrtle leaves attached to *lulav.*

Hag Sameiah. "Happy holiday." Festival greeting.

Hakafot. Processions around sanctuary with Torah scroll on Sukkot and Simhat Torah.

Ḥatan Beresheet. "Bridegroom of Genesis." Special honor on Simḥat Torah of being called up for first *sidrah* in annual cycle of Torah readings.

Ḥatan Torah. "Bridegroom of Torah." Special honor on Simḥat Torah of being called up for last *sidrah* in annual cycle of Torah readings.

Ḥol Hamoed. Intermediate days of a festival; work is permitted.

Lulav. Palm branch, one of the Four Species.

S'khakh. Greens covering the roof of the *sukkah*.

Sukkah. Small booth used on Sukkot.

Yizkor. Memorial prayer for the dead recited on or near last day of every major festival.

Ḥanukkah

Al HaNissim. Special prayer of deliverance.

Antiochus. Syrian king who forbade Jews to practice their religion.

Dreidel (*sevivon* in Hebrew). Four-sided top used in Hanukkah games.

Hallel. Psalms praising God recited on Hanukkah, Rosh Hodesh, and Pilgrimage Festivals.

Ḥanukkah. Festival of Dedication, occurring on twenty-fifth of Kislev and lasting for eight days.

Ḥanukkah gelt. Money given to children as Hanukkah gift.

Ḥanukkiah. Hanukkah candelabrum.

Kislev. Hebrew month in which Hanukkah begins.

Latkes. See Food Terms.

Maoz Tzur. "Rock of Ages." Popular hymn sung on Hanukkah.

Nun, Gimel, Hay, and *Shin.* Hebrew letters on the dreidel. They stand for the Hebrew words *nes gadol hayah sham,* meaning "a great miracle happened there."

Shamash. Special "servant" candle used to light the other candles in the *hanukkiah.*

Tevet. Hebrew month in which Hanukkah ends.

Purim

Adar. Hebrew month during which Purim occurs.

Ahasuerus. King of Persia involved in Purim story.

Esther. Wife of Ahasuerus and heroine of Purim story. The Scroll of Esther is read during the Purim service.

Feast of Lots. Another name for Purim.

Gragger (ra'ashan in Hebrew). Noisemaker used during the Megillah reading to drown out Haman's name.

Hadassah. Esther's Hebrew name.

Haman. Prime minister of Ahasuerus. He tried to persuade king to permit pogrom against Persian Jews; instead, he was hung.

Hamantashen. See Food Terms.

Matanot l'evyonim. Gifts to the poor on Purim.

Mordecai. Cousin of Esther and hero of Purim story.

Pur. Lot cast to determine one's fate. Name of holiday comes from the plural form, *purim*.

Seudah. Special feast associated with a holiday or Jewish life-cycle event.

Shushan. City where story of Purim took place.

Shushan Purim. The day after Purim (the fifteenth of Adar), ordained by the Jews in Persia's capital and in walled cities.

Ta'anit Esther. Fast of Esther, observed just before Purim from dawn to dusk, in commemoration of the fast Esther imposed on herself.

Vashti. King Ahasuerus' rebellious queen.

Passover

Afikoman. Piece of matzah hidden at beginning of Seder, to be found by the children.

Bedikat Ḥametz. Search for unleavened bread on night before Passover.

Beitzah. See Food Terms.

Biur Ḥametz. Burning of ḥametz on morning before Passover.

Four Questions. Questions asked by youngest child during early part of Seder.

Ḥad Gadya. "One kid." A favorite Seder song.

Haggadah. Book used at Seder service.

Hametz. See Food Terms.

Haroset. See Food Terms.

Karpas. See Food Terms.

Mah Nishtanah. Opening words of Four Questions.

Ma-ot Hittim. Special matzah fund used to help needy before Passover.

Maror. See Food Terms.

Matzah. See Food Terms.

Moadim Lesimhah "Joyous festival." Festival greeting.

Nisan. Month when Exodus from Egypt took place. Passover begins on fourteen of Nisan.

Seder. Festive meal and ceremony held on first two nights of Passover (first night only in Israel and for Reform Jews).

Zeroa. See Food Terms.

Shavuot

Akdamut. Special liturgical poem read during Shavuot services.

Bikkurim. First fruits brought to Temple as Shavuot offering.

Blintz. See Food Terms.

Feast of Weeks. Another name for Shavuot.

Sivan. Hebrew month in which Shavuot occurs.

Tikkun Leil Shavuot. Study session on night of Shavuot.

Jewish Food Terms

Beitzah. Roasted egg on Seder plate, a symbol of life.

Blintz. Thin crepe-like pancake filled with cottage cheese or fruit. Often served on Shavuot.

Borsht. Beet soup often served with sour cream or boiled potato.

Ḥallah. Braided bread used on Sabbaths and festivals.

Fleishig (Yiddish). Foods prepared with meat or meat products; in accordance with the dietary laws, they may not be eaten with dairy (milchig) foods.

Gefilte fish. Stuffed fish, often served as first course of Sabbath or holiday meal.

Ḥametz. Foods containing leavened grains; forbidden on Passover.

Ḥaroset. Mixture of apples, cinnamon, nuts, and wine served on Passover, symbolizing mortar used to make bricks in Egypt.

Hamantashen. Triangular pockets of dough filled with poppy seeds or jam served on Purim.

Karpas. Greens (usually parsley) on Seder plate, symbolizing spring. Some people use potatoes for *karpas.*

Kneidel. Matzah-meal dumpling, often added to chicken broth. Sometimes called matzah ball.

Kosher. Refers to foods that are fit to be eaten according to Jewish dietary laws.

Kreplach. Triangular dumplings often filled with meat and served with soup.

Kugel. Noodle or potato pudding.

Latke (*levivah* in Hebrew). Potato pancake, traditionally eaten on Hanukkah.

Maror. Bitter herbs, usually horseradish, served at Passover Seder.

Matzah. Unleavened bread eaten during Passover.

Milchig (Yiddish). Foods prepared with milk or other dairy products; in accordance with dietary laws, they may not be eaten with, or immediately after, meat (*fleishig*) foods.

Pareve (Yiddish). Foods that are neither *fleishig* nor *milchig* but neutral according to dietary laws; e.g., fruits and vegetables.

Zeroa. Roasted lamb shankbone symbolizing Passover sacrifice in ancient Temple.

Life-cycle Terms

Birth And Education

Bar Mitzvah (masc.), *Bat Mitzvah* (fem). One who is responsible for observing the mitzvot (religious commandments). For boys this occurs at age thirteen, for girls at age twelve.

Brit Milah. Circumcision ceremony occurring on eighth day after birth of Jewish boy.

Confirmation. Ceremony often tied to Shavuot in which teenagers confirm their acceptance of Judaism.

Kohen. Descendant of the ancient priestly tribe. Conducts *Pidyon HaBen* ceremony for firstborn and receives honor of first aliyah at services.

Kvater (masc.), *Kvaterin* (fem.). Godfather and godmother, appointed at time of circumcision.

Mohel (masc.), *Mohelet* (fem.). Person who performs surgery during ritual circumcision.

Pidyon HaBen. Ceremony for redemption of firstborn.

Sandek. Person who holds child at ritual circumcision.

Simhat Bat. Naming ceremony of newborn Jewish girl.

Shalom Zakhar/Shalom Nekeivah. Ceremony welcoming newborn Jewish child (boy or girl), often held on first Friday evening after birth.

Marriage

Aufruf. Calling of the groom-to-be (and often of bride-to-be) to Torah on Shabbat before wedding day.

Badeken. Ceremony for veiling bride.

Erusin. Betrothal.

Get. Religious divorce, required to terminate a Jewish marriage.

Ḥatan. Groom.

Ḥuppah. Wedding canopy under which bride and groom stand during wedding ceremony. May consist of a *tallit* (prayer-shawl) and poles.

Kallah. Bride.

Ketubah. Marriage contract.

Kiddushin. Wedding.

Mikvah. Ritual bath.

Nesuin. Marriage.

Shadkhan. Jewish match-maker.

Sheva Berakhot. Seven wedding blessings.

Tenaim. Stipulations concerning proposed marriage.

Yiḥud. "Unchaperoned togetherness"; time when bride and groom are together and alone immediately following wedding ceremony.

Death And Mourning

Alav Hashalom. Hebrew for "May he rest in peace."

Aleha Hashalom. Hebrew for "May she rest in peace."

Eil Malei. Prayer for peace of departed soul.

Ḥevra Kaddisha. "Holy Society," group responsible for preparing body for burial.

Keriah. Tearing of garment as sign of mourning.

Mourner's Kaddish. Traditional prayer affirming life, recited by mourners.

Onen. Designation of mourner prior to funeral; as onen, one is exempted from the performance of religious obligations.

Sheloshim. First thirty days of mourning period.

Shivah. "Seven." First seven days of mourning.

Taharah. Ritual cleansing of deceased by *Hevra Kaddisha* prior to funeral.

Unveiling. Service marking consecration of tombstone.

Yahrzeit. Anniversary of death.

Yizkor. Memorial prayers recited on Shemini Atzeret, Passover, Shavuot, and Yom Kippur.

GENERAL TERMS

Ashkenazim. Jews who follow traditions of northern and central Europe.

Aveirah. Transgression of God's law.

Barukh Hashem. "May God be blessed." Expression having effect of "Thank God, I'm fine" in response to polite inquiries such as "How are you?"

Bet Din. Court of Jewish law.

Bikkur Holim. Visiting the sick, an important religious obligation.

B'nai Yisrael. "Children of Israel." The Jewish people.

Codes. Books of Jewish law.

Eretz Yisrael. The land of Israel.

Galut. Dispersion of Jews throughout the world. Also called Diaspora.

Gemara. Major rabbinic commentary on the Mishnah, the major part of the Talmud.

Ger. A convert.

Halakhah. Jewish law.

Hatikvah. "The Hope." Israel's national anthem.

Ḥevra. A fellowship of friends.

Ḥutzpah. Audacity, nerve.

Kashrut. The Jewish dietary laws.

Klezmer. Eastern European instrumental music.

Leḥayim. "To Life." Toast offered before drinking wine or liquor.

Mazal tov. Expression meaning "good luck" or "congratulations."

Mentsch (Yiddish). A decent, admirable person.

Mishnah. First postbiblical code of Jewish law, elaborated upon by Gemara.

Mitzvah. A religious commandment. Judaism has 613 of them.

Naches. Joy, often from children and grandchildren.

Pushke. Tzedakah container in which coins are placed for charity.

Rabbinical Assembly. International professional organization of Conservative rabbis.

Responsa. Formal written replies to questions on Jewish law by qualified legal authorities.

Rosh Ḥodesh. Beginning of new Jewish month.

Sephardim. Jews who follow traditions which originated in Spain and North Africa.

Shalom Bayit. Family harmony.

Shulḥan Arukh. Authoritative Code of Jewish Law written by Joseph Caro (sixteenth century).

Simḥah. Joyous occasion, often associated with a life-cycle event, e.g., a Bar/Bat Mitzvah or a wedding.

Talmud. Compendium of Jewish law, consisting of Mishnah and Gemara.

Tanakh. The Bible, consisting of the Torah, Prophets, and Writings.

Torah. (1) The Five Books of Moses (Genesis, Exodus, Leviticus, Numbers, Deuteronomy). (2) The scroll kept in the ark from which a portion is read at services each week.

Tzaddik. A righteous person.

Tzedakah. Deeds of kindness (charity).

Yarmulke (kippah in Hebrew). Skullcap.

Yom Tov. Festival.